THE ANTONINE WALL

THE ANTONINE WALL

A Handbook to the Roman Wall
between Forth and Clyde and a
Guide to its surviving remains

BY

ANNE S. ROBERTSON

Professor Emerita of Roman Archaeology
and Former Keeper of the Hunter Coin Cabinet,
University of Glasgow

GLASGOW ARCHAEOLOGICAL SOCIETY

1979

First Published 1960
Second Printing 1963
Third Printing 1968
Fourth Printing 1970
Revised Edition 1973
New Edition 1979

PRINTED IN GREAT BRITAIN BY
T. AND A. CONSTABLE LTD., EDINBURGH

FOREWORD

IT is now almost 20 years since the first edition of Professor Robertson's Handbook to the Antonine Wall was published under the auspices of the Glasgow Archaeological Society. Since then it has run through four further impressions, in each of which new material has been incorporated to keep pace with the progress of research on the Wall. Once again stocks of the volume have become exhausted, so that a new printing has become necessary. As early as the third printing in 1968, the then president of the society wrote that it was a problem to decide when a new printing became a new edition; now, 11 years later, the author has decided that the extent of the alterations involved merits this change in nomenclature. Besides the incorporation of material from the important new excavation at the Bearsden fort, which came just too late for incorporation in the last impression, and from recent work at Croy Hill and Seabegs Wood, the measurements shown in the text and in most of the plans have been converted from the imperial to the metric scale. The only exceptions to this are those fort-plans re-drawn for the first edition by the late Mr. T. M. Lighbody, five of which were first published in the *Proceedings of the Society of Antiquaries of Scotland* and are reproduced by kind permission of the Council of the Society. These have been preserved in their original form as a tribute to his fine draughtsmanship, as it was technically impossible to superimpose a metric scale on them.

The author wishes to acknowledge the help of many others who have assisted her at various stages in the work, many of them members of the Glasgow Archaeological Society. These include two life members, Professor J. K. S. St. Joseph and Professor E. Birley, for information respectively about temporary camps and about the Fourth

Cohort of Gauls at Castlehill. Dr. D. J. Breeze provided a plan of his excavations at Bearsden, Mr W. S. Hanson one of structures at Croy Hill, and Mr. L. J. F. Keppie of the fortlet at Seabegs Wood. Mr. G. Maxwell of the Royal Commission provided information on the recently discovered Flavian forts at Drumquhassle and Mollins and about temporary camps on the Wall. Mrs. J. G. Scott (Margaret Scott) provided drawings of two distance slabs and a reconstruction drawing of the Antonine Wall, and permission to reproduce these was given by Professor F. Willett of the Hunterian Museum. Mr. R. W. Feachem drew the endpaper map specially for the handbook, and Mr. M. Jones supplied notes to the author of the present state of the remains.

It is a privilege, as President of the Society, to contribute the preface to this new edition, and to express its appreciation to Professor Robertson for her continuing willingness to bring up to date her account of the Wall. In this year particularly, when the International Congress of Roman Frontier Studies is coming to Scotland for the first time, it is especially appropriate that the Society, which since its foundation in 1856 has been concerned with the study of the Wall, should be able to make this handbook available.

J. A. F. THOMSON
President, 1979

THE ANTONINE WALL

THE ANTONINE WALL formed the most north-westerly frontier of the Roman Empire. It ran from sea to sea across the narrowest part of Scotland, where—in the words of the late first-century historian, Tacitus—the firths of " Clota and Bodotria, being carried far inland by tides from opposite seas, are separated by but a narrow strip of land ".

The only written information about the building of the Antonine Wall which has come down to us from Roman times is one sentence: *nam et Britannos per Lollium Urbicum vicit legatum alio muro cespiticio summotis barbaris ducto.* " For he (i.e. the emperor Antoninus Pius), conquered the Britons through Lollius Urbicus the governor (i.e. of Britain), and after driving back the barbarians, built another wall, this time of turf ". Inscribed stones found at Corbridge, Northumberland, prove that Lollius Urbicus was in Britain as governor as early as the year A.D. 139. His campaigns against the northern barbarians and the subsequent building of the Antonine Wall must therefore have taken place within a few years of that date.

The army of Lollius Urbicus doubtless moved north-wards along the same two main natural routes into Scotland which an earlier Roman invader, Agricola, had used 60 years before on his way to the Forth-Clyde isthmus. One of these routes was by way of the Tweed and Lauderdale to the Forth, and the other ran up Annandale and on to upper Clydesdale. Lower Clydesdale, too, featured in the Antonine system although not apparently in the Flavian road system as developed after Agricola's campaigns. In the Antonine period, forts were built not only at Castle-dykes, near Lanark, but also at Bothwellhaugh, near Hamilton. A road linked these forts and must have continued north towards the Forth-Clyde isthmus (Figs. 1, 2).

The troublesome North Britons were forced back into their own mountains, and a penetrative road, guarded by forts, was driven far into Perthshire. The irreconcilable elements in S.W. Scotland were kept in check by a network

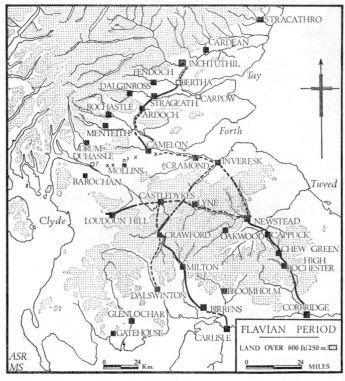

FIGURE I. Map showing Flavian routes and permanent sites. The open squares mark sites whose Flavian date, although probable, is not absolutely certain.

of roads, forts and fortlets, probably linked with a harbour on the Solway.

As a result of the victory won by Lollius Urbicus over the North Britons, the emperor Antoninus Pius received an acclamation as *imperator*—victorious commander-in-chief—

either at the end of A.D. 142 or early in A.D. 143. Bronze coins of Antoninus Pius commemorating the victory and the acclamation have on the reverse side the figure of Britannia subdued.

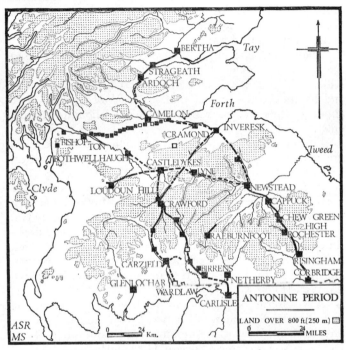

FIGURE 2. Map showing Antonine routes and permanent sites. The open squares mark sites whose Antonine date, although probable, is not absolutely certain.

These coins, minted in late A.D. 142 or early A.D. 143, determine the date of Lollius Urbicus' campaigns in North Britain, and also provide an approximate date, about A.D. 142 or 143, for the building of the Antonine Wall which followed swiftly thereafter. The location of the Antonine Wall was established once and for all in 1698, when a fragment of a Roman inscribed stone was detected at Balmuildy, on the line of a turf wall, the remains of which

7

could still be seen running across the Forth-Clyde isthmus. This stone recorded building work carried out by the Second Legion in the reign of Antoninus Pius, and in the governorship of Lollius Urbicus. So excited was the early eighteenth-century antiquary, Alexander Gordon, by its significance that he called it " the most invaluable Jewel of Antiquity, that ever was found in the Island of Britain ".

The eastern end of the Wall was at Bridgeness, close to the present Bridgeness Tower. On the west it ended at Old Kilpatrick at a point now obliterated by a railway line and by the Forth-Clyde Canal. The Wall was therefore about 37 miles (c. 60 km.) long, that is about 40 Roman miles.

For the greater part of its length it clung to the southern slopes of the valley of the Forth-Clyde isthmus, with an uninterrupted outlook to the bottom of the valley and across its streams and bogs to the threatening hills on the north. Very rarely did the line dip into a hollow, and then only when passing from one ridge to another. At only two points had the line to be carried across rivers of any size— the Avon near its east end and the Kelvin near its west end. At only one point, west of Falkirk—so far as is at present known—did a major Roman route run northwards through the Wall (Fig. 3).

A long series of excavations has been conducted on the Antonine Wall at intervals between 1890 and the present day, first of all by the Antonine Wall Committee of the Glasgow Archaeological Society, later under the auspices of the Society of Antiquaries of Scotland or of the Hunterian Museum, and more recently by the Department of the Environment, or the Scottish Development Department. These excavations have proved that for the greater part of its length, the Antonine Wall had, as the Roman writer said, been built of turf, or to be accurate, of rows of aligned turves which pencilled the face of every section " with their ineffaceable parallel dark lines " of decayed vegetation. Although literally a *murus cespiticius*—a turf wall—the Antonine Wall was underpinned by a stone base, formed of

8

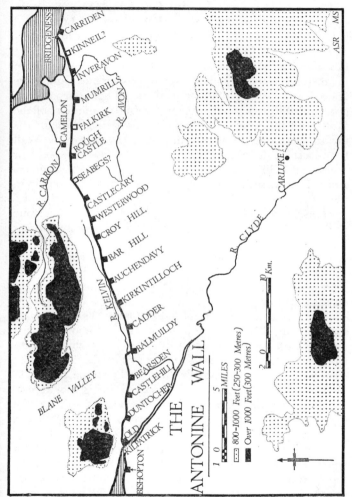

THE
ANTONINE WALL

CARRIDEN
KINNEIL?
INVERAVON
MUMRILLS
FALKIRK
ROUGH CASTLE
SEABEGS?
CASTLECARY
WESTERWOOD
CROY HILL
BAR HILL
AUCHENDAVY
KIRKINTILLOCH
CADDER
BALMUILDY
BEARSDEN
CASTLEHILL
DUNTOCHER
OLD KILPATRICK
BISHOPTON

BRIDGENESS

R. CARRON
CAMELON
R. AVON
R. KELVIN
BLANE VALLEY
R. CLYDE
CARLUKE

MILES
1 0   5

⋯⋯ 800-1000 Feet (250-300 Metres)
■■ Over 1000 Feet (300 Metres)

10 Km.
2 0

ASR MS

FIGURE 3

two outer rows of squared kerb-stones, with a mass of rough unshaped stones packed in between. This stone base had a width of 14 feet (4·3 m.) or more, for example on the eastern slope of Bar Hill, where it was 15½ feet (4·7 m.) broad, and at some points on Croy Hill, and on Golden Hill, Duntocher, where it was 16 feet (4·8 m.) wide. At intervals, the stone base had culverts incorporated in it. These were formed of huge stones roughly squared on the inner face, and were floored and covered with stone slabs. Their purpose was apparently to carry off water gathering at the foot of the Wall, and moisture which might seep down through the turf superstructure. At certain places, too, where the Wall lay on a steep slope, the stone foundation was " stepped " or " terraced " to increase the stability of the turf super-structure. At several points there is evidence of repair to the base.

The turf wall did not rise straight upwards, like a stone wall, but its sides were " battered " or sloped inwards as they rose higher for the sake of stability. In at least one section cut through the Antonine Wall, on Croy Hill, the " batter " or slope on the south side of the Wall was clearly visible. It may well be that the slope was somewhat steeper on the north or enemy side.

The turf superstructure of the Antonine Wall is not now standing anywhere to a height of more than about 5-6 feet (1·5-1·8 m.). An attempt to estimate its original height, based on the evidence of its average width at the base, 14 feet (4·3 m.), and its probable " batter " or slope, has led to the conclusion that it may have reached a height of at least 10 feet (3 m.), with a width of about 6 feet (1·8 m.) at the top—affording enough space for two patrols to pass one another.

The flat top would probably have been covered by a wooden duckboard walk, and along the north edge of the top there would probably have been a wooden breastwork or palisade. Access to the top of the Wall may have been by way of wooden ladders, either movable or fixed, although no trace of these has survived. The whole structure, stone base, turf wall and wooden breastwork, might well have attained a height of at least 16 feet (4·8 m.) (Fig. 4A).

Whether the stretches of the Wall where the stone base was well over 14 feet (4·3 m.) wide reached a still greater height, is of course unknown, and will indeed probably never be known. An increase in the width (and possibly in the height) of the Wall at certain points may well, however, have had a very good reason behind it. The construction of the Wall by different working squads is one possible

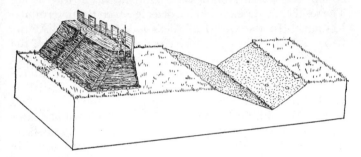

FIGURE 4A. Reconstruction drawing of the Antonine Wall and Ditch.

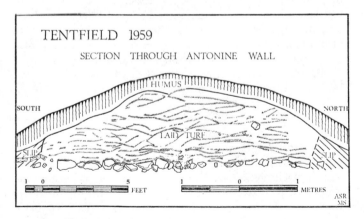

FIGURE 4B

reason. The natural strength or weakness of the line at certain points is another.

To the north of the Wall there ran a Ditch, often approaching a width of about 40 feet (12 m.) and a depth of about 12 feet (3·6 m.). Its dimensions were, however, less impressive in certain areas, usually at or near forts on the Wall, for example at Mumrills, Castlecary, Balmuildy, Bearsden, Duntocher and Old Kilpatrick.

At one point, on the eastern shoulder of Croy Hill, an 80-foot (25 m.) stretch of the Ditch was never dug at all. The solid rock appears to have defeated even the determined Romans. In the words of Alexander Gordon: " At the Croe Hill, there is a great Piece of a Rock rises out of the Ditch of the Vallum, and serves, as it were, for a Bridge to pass from the one Side to the other ". So persistent have been the efforts of the diggers elsewhere in driving their Ditch through intractable ground that it comes as a surprise to find them failing at this one point. The refusal of a later eighteenth-century antiquary, William Maitland, to believe that they did fail made him the author of a remarkable statement: " As in this neighbourhood appear the great pains taken by the Romans in erecting a passage for the ditch through rocks, it cannot be reasonably imagined they would leave a rock undemolished in this part. Now as I am, for certain reasons (too long to be inserted in this place), of opinion that rocks vegetate, the rock here, by its form, must have sprung up since the making of the said ditch." A shorter stretch of Ditch, 10-12 feet (3-3·6 m.) long, was left uncompleted just to the north of Castle Hill, east of Bar Hill.

The Ditch was V-shaped, with angles of both scarp and counterscarp approximating to 30°, and in some places at least it had a square drainage channel in the bottom. At some points too the edges of the Ditch were hardened with a setting of large stones. It was not intended, as is sometimes supposed, to hold water like a moat. In the plain-spoken words of the nineteenth-century Antonine Wall Report of the Glasgow Archaeological Society: " The nature of its construction, and the absence of any effort to keep either the bottom or the top of the banks at one level for any distance, are fatal to the supposition, which may be dismissed as pure nonsense ".

The upcast from the Ditch was thrown out on its north side, and was usually flattened out, so as not to provide cover for an enemy. At some points, however, where the Ditch was on a northward slope, the upcast was not levelled but was left to form the so-called " outer mound " of the Glasgow Archaeological Society's Antonine Wall Report.

The berm, or space between Wall and Ditch, was seldom less than 20 feet (6 m.) wide and in some places was much more. At one place, on the rocky face of Croy Hill, the berm attained a width of well over 100 feet (30 m.).

To the south of the Wall, at an average distance of 40-50 yards (36-46 m.), there ran a road—the Military Way. It was 16-18 feet (4·8-5·4 m.) wide, with a distinct camber, so that rainwater would drain away quickly into gutters running along the sides.

The Wall, Ditch and Military Way formed the continuous elements of the Antonine frontier. The construction of this great barrier was carried out by squads of highly trained legionary troops, Roman citizens all. They were doubtless protected from attack while at work by units of auxiliaries, lighter-armed, more expendable, non-citizen troops, and they may have had enforced assistance in the unskilled tasks of fetching and carrying from native Britons.

There have been recorded from the line of the Antonine Wall at least eighteen legionary tablets or " distance slabs ", set up by working squads of legionaries to commemorate the distance or length of the Wall which they had completed. These distance slabs show that each of the three legions then stationed in Britain was called on to supply men for the construction of the Antonine Wall (and probably for the campaigns against the North Britons which preceded it). The Sixth Legion, stationed at York, and the Twentieth Legion, whose fortress was at Chester, supplied detachments only—numbering perhaps 1,000 men each out of the total legionary strength of over 5,000 men. The Second Legion, on the other hand, whose headquarters were at Caerleon in South Wales, appears to have been present on the Antonine Wall in full strength.

Ten distance slabs found in the four-mile (6·4 km.) sector at the western end of the Wall, from Castlehill to Old Kilpatrick, show that this sector was built in six separate lengths, each measured in Roman feet, for the completion of which the Second, the Sixth and the Twentieth Legions supplied two working squads each. The Twentieth Legion is actually represented on this sector by five stones forming two sets of duplicates, thus indicating that the completion of a length was marked by at least one distance slab at each end. Another Twentieth Legion slab from the Castlehill-Old Kilpatrick sector has an unfinished inscription (Fig. 5).

The eight distance slabs which have survived from the 33-mile (53 km.) long sector from Castlehill to the Forth recorded the completion of much longer stretches of the Wall, each measured in Roman paces. (The Roman pace equalled 5 linear feet (1·5 m.).) These eight slabs included two pairs of duplicates, set up by men of the Second and Sixth Legions. To these eight easterly distance slabs may be added two fragments of a large tablet found east of Arniebog which probably had been a distance slab, since it bore the figure of a kneeling captive, a not uncommon figure on distance slabs, for example of the Twentieth Legion.

Sir George Macdonald, the greatest recent authority on the Antonine Wall, explained the change in the unit of measurement at Castlehill by supposing that the building of the Wall was begun from the east, and was expected to be completed in nine lengths or sectors, each of which was assigned to a particular working squad. The working squad assigned to the fifth length, however, found itself confronted on Croy Hill with the task of cutting the Antonine Ditch through solid rock and lagged far behind the other squads. By the time the ensuing confusion was

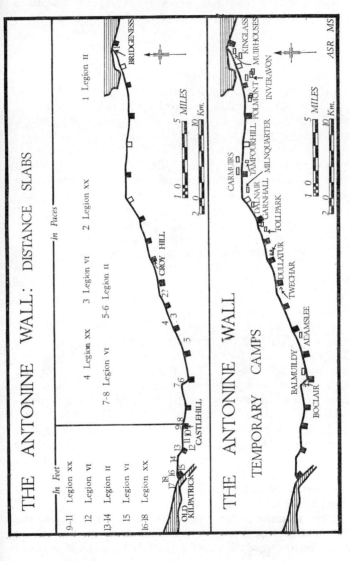

THE ANTONINE WALL: DISTANCE SLABS

— *in Feet* —

— *in Paces* —

9-11	Legion XX	1	Legion II
12	Legion VI		
13-14	Legion II	2	Legion XX
15	Legion VI	3	Legion VI
16-18	Legion XX	4	Legion XX
		5-6	Legion II
		7-8	Legion VI

OLD KILPATRICK

17 18 16 14 15 13 12 11 10 9

CASTLEHILL

8 7 6 5 4 3 2? CROY HILL

BRIDGENESS

MILES
1   0   5
1   0   2
10 Km.

THE ANTONINE WALL

TEMPORARY CAMPS

BALMUILDY
BOCLAIR
ALAMSLEE
TWECHAR
DULLATUR
TOLLPARK
GARNHALL
DALNAIR
MILNQUARTER
TAMFOURHILL
CARMUIRS
POLMONT
INVERAVON
MUIRHOUSES
KINGLASS

MILES
1   0   5
1   0   2
10 Km.

ASR MS

FIGURE 5

straightened out there was an odd sector, from Castlehill to the Clyde, left over at the western end of the Wall. This, Sir George suggested, was subdivided into six short stretches, built by six separate working squads, two drawn from each of the three legions.

Mr. S. N. Miller, however, another authority of the greatest discernment, put forward the theory that the reason why, west of Castlehill, the working squads were allotted short instead of long stretches, and so were in closer touch with one another, was simply because " here they were working under the immediate threat of ' assaults and interruptions ' from the Kilpatrick Hills. It was a sector which they would be anxious to finish off as quickly as possible and where they would have good reason to take special precations for their security ".

As the map of the findspots of distance slabs shows, there is not a complete enough series surviving from the 33-mile (53 km.) long stretch of the Wall from the Forth westwards to Castlehill to prove how that part of the work was organised, or to indicate why the change in the unit of measurement, from paces to feet, or from feet to paces, became advisable.

Among the most outstanding distance slabs are the two which marked the eastern and western ends of the Wall. The Bridgeness slab recorded the completion of 4,652 paces by the Second Legion. The inscription is flanked on the right by a scene representing the *suovetaurilia*, a ceremonial sacrifice used to inaugurate a particularly important undertaking, and marked by the slaughter of a pig, a sheep and a bull. On the left side is the figure of a Roman cavalryman riding over four barbarians. Found in 1868, the Bridgeness slab at once attracted the interest of Dr. John Buchanan, whose keen eye enabled him thus to describe the features of the Roman horseman: " The face is that of a middle-aged man, and the expression determined ".

The distance slab found, some time before 1684, at the west end of the Wall, at Old Kilpatrick on the Clyde, recorded the completion of 4,411 feet by a detachment of

16

FIGURE 6A. Twentieth Legion distance slab from Old Kilpatrick.

FIGURE 6B. Twentieth Legion distance slab from Hutcheson Hill.

17

the Twentieth Legion (Fig. 6A). The inscription is partly enclosed in a temple façade within which the goddess Victory, holding a laurel-wreath and palm-branch, is seated at rest.

The most remarkable of all the known distance slabs was found as recently as 1969, on Hutcheson Hill, west of Castlehill, Bearsden. It records the completion of 3,000 feet of the Wall by a detachment of the Twentieth Legion.

The inscription has been skilfully arranged within an elaborate architectural framework, with features reminiscent of the much simpler temple façade of the Old Kilpatrick distance slab. The Hutcheson Hill slab may represent either a triumphal arch or the shrine of the standards. The central niche or panel encloses a female figure holding out a round object, probably a wreath, to an eagle held by an aquilifer. The panels on either side contain kneeling captives. Below the central panel there is a wild boar, running right (Fig. 6B).

Twentieth Legion stones usually bear the legionary emblem, a wild boar. Second Legion distance slabs often have a capricorn or a pegasus or both, these being emblems of the Second Legion, but on Sixth Legion stones no legionary emblem appears. Why, is not known.

Two Sixth Legion stones, one found in 1812 to the east of Duntocher, and the other found before 1695 between Duntocher and Old Kilpatrick, have preserved the name by which the Antonine Wall was known, at least officially, to the men, or some of the men, who built it. It is described on these two stones as *opus valli*, " the work of the vallum, or rampart ".

It is far from certain exactly how much is meant by *opus valli*. So little is known of the working arrangements of the legionary squads on the Antonine Wall that there is not sure ground for assuming that a squad which erected a certain stretch of the Wall also dug the same stretch of the Ditch and laid down the corresponding stretch of the Military Way. Nor indeed can it be assumed that Wall builders, Ditch diggers and road makers always worked exactly neck and neck, whether they came from the same squad or not. It is this uncertainty which prevents un-hesitating acceptance of Sir George Macdonald's suggestion that the digging of the Antonine Ditch through solid rock on Croy Hill would have had the effect of throwing the whole working-programme out of gear.

It is even more uncertain how long the construction of the Antonine Wall, Ditch and Military Way would have taken. There are so many incalculable, inconstant factors; for example, the distances over which good building stone and suitable turf had to be sought and transported, the extent to which the work was hampered by hostile attacks, and, not least, the weather, which at its most severe would slow up even the toughest legionaries. It may be that in *very* favourable conditions the barrier could have been completed in a long campaigning season, a period of about six months.

In any case, the legionary builders were long enough at their construction work on the Antonine Wall to require living accommodation while so engaged. Within the last few years Professor J. K. S. St. Joseph has discovered, by observation from the air, eighteen Roman temporary camps on the Forth-Clyde line. Three others have recently been found through aerial survey by the Royal Commission on Ancient and Historical Monuments (Scotland). The ram-part and ditch which formed the defences of the camps have long been obliterated, so that no traces are ordinarily visible on the ground. From the air the outlines of the camps may be seen by differences in the colour of the vegetation growing over them. Most of these camps lay to the south of the Wall, within a quarter of a mile (·4 km.) of it. Three camps lay less than half-a-mile (·8 km.) to the north of the Wall, the largest being the camp near Balmuildy, about 11 acres (4·4 h.) in internal area.

Although none of these camps has been securely dated, their situation and distribution suggest that they may have been the labour camps of men engaged in the building of the Antonine Wall. Indeed, it may be possible to relate these camps to the stretches of Wall assigned to the various legionary working squads (Fig. 5).

Structural remains of forts on the Antonine Wall have been discovered through excavation (archaeological or otherwise) at thirteen sites on the line: Mumrills, Rough Castle, Castlecary, Westerwood, Croy Hill, Bar Hill, Auchendavy (where the excavations for the Forth-Clyde Canal brought to light many Roman finds), Kirkintilloch, Cadder, Balmuildy, Bearsden, Duntocher and Old Kilpatrick. The discovery of a Roman altar and other Roman material at another site, Castlehill, long ago established it too as the site of an Antonine Wall fort, and this has more recently been confirmed through the detection by Professor St. Joseph from the air of the south ditches and south-east angle of the fort.

The distribution of the known forts along the line of the Antonine Wall suggests that the Roman plan *when complete* called for forts at every 2 miles (3·2 km.) from Forth to Clyde. If it be assumed that Antonine Wall forts did finally occur at two-mile intervals, there should be forts still awaiting discovery or re-discovery at the east end of the Wall at Bridgeness (unless its place was taken by the fort at Carriden, less than a mile (1·6 km.) to the south-east), at Kinneil (somewhere near Kinneil House), at Inveravon (where a Roman structure has now been found), at Falkirk (now buried beneath the modern town), and near Bonnybridge or Seabegs (Fig. 7).

The known forts were all situated on ground which in Roman times afforded a very wide outlook to north and usually indeed in all directions. The possibility cannot yet be discounted that some of these sites were used *for some purpose* 60 years earlier by Agricola when, according to Tacitus, he strengthened the isthmus by garrisons or small forts. Remains of a small fort, with heavily silted and overgrown ditches, have been found lying under the Antonine Wall fort on Bar Hill, and askew to the Wall line. Mumrills, Castlecary, Cadder, Balmuildy and Old Kilpatrick have provided evidence in the form of glass,

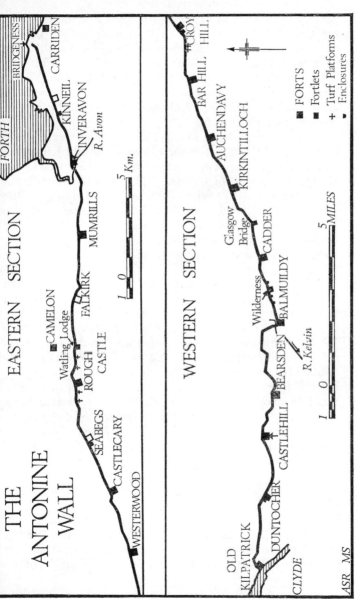

THE
ANTONINE
WALL

EASTERN SECTION

FORTH
BRIDGENESS
CARRIDEN
KINNEIL
INVERAVON
R. Avon
MUMRILLS
CAMELON
Watling Lodge
FALKIRK
ROUGH CASTLE
SEABEGS
CASTLECARY
WESTERWOOD

1   0   5 Km.

WESTERN SECTION

CROY
BAR HILL
AUCHENDAVY
KIRKINTILLOCH
Gasgow Bridge
CADDER
Wilderness
BALMUILDY
R. Kelvin
BEARSDEN
CASTLEHILL
DUNTOCHER
OLD KILPATRICK
CLYDE

■ FORTS
■ Fortlets
+ Turf Platforms
▶ Enclosures

1   0   5 MILES

ASR MS

FIGURE 7

pottery or short-lived bronze coins of the first century A.D., for the probable presence of Agricolan troops, *in some capacity*. In 1978, a newly discovered small fort at Mollins, $2\frac{1}{2}$ miles (4 km.) south of Bar Hill, proved to be of Flavian date. North of the isthmus, at Camelon, a Flavian fort has long been known. South-west of the isthmus, at Barochan, an Agricolan fort has recently been discovered by Mr. F. Newall (Fig. 1).

The Antonine Wall forts which have been extensively excavated all faced to the north, except for Old Kilpatrick which faced north-west, and for Cadder which faced east. Except in the case of Cadder, and Bar Hill (which lay a short distance south of the Wall), and tiny Duntocher, the Military Way passed through each fort as its *via principalis*. It was also, however, provided with a series of loops, or by-passes, skirting the southern defences of forts, so that traffic not intended for a particular fort could make a detour to avoid passing through it.

The excavated forts varied greatly in size, ranging in internal area from Mumrills (6·5 acres: 2·6 h.) to Rough Castle (1 acre: ·4 h.) and Duntocher (·5 acre: ·2 h.) (Fig. 8). Only five or six of the forts could have held whole cohorts of auxiliary troops. Mumrills could have held a cohort 1,000 strong. Old Kilpatrick (4·2 acres: 1·7 h.), Balmuildy (4 acres: 1·6 h.), Castlecary (3·5 acres: 1·4 h.), Bar Hill (3·2 acres: 1·3 h.), and possibly Cadder (2·8 acres: 1·12 h.) could have held cohorts 500 strong. The remaining forts, Bearsden (2·3 acres: ·9 h.), Westerwood (1·95 acres: ·78 h.), Croy Hill (1·5 acres: ·6 h.), Rough Castle and Duntocher must have had smaller garrisons. A cohort may have been subdivided to provide garrisons for two or more forts.

Several forts have in fact provided evidence, in the form of building inscriptions, altars or tombstones, for the presence there of men from specific auxiliary units.

Mumrills had men from a Cavalry Regiment of Tungri and the Second Cohort of Thracians, each 500 strong; Castlecary had men from the First Cohort of Tungri and the

First Loyal Cohort of Vardulli, *equitata*, each 1,000 strong; Bar Hill had men from the First Cohort of Baetasii and the First Cohort of Hamii, each 500 strong; and Rough Castle had men from the Sixth Cohort of Nervii, 500 strong. One other auxiliary cohort known to have served on the Antonine Wall was the Fourth Cohort of Gauls (*equitata*), 500 strong, whose commander set up an altar at Castlehill, Bearsden.

An altar found in 1969 at Old Kilpatrick had been dedicated by the First Cohort of Baetasii, which was at one time stationed at Bar Hill.

Of these auxiliary units, the Fourth Cohort of Gauls was enlisted in Gaul, and the Vardulli in Spain, while the Baetasii, Nervii and Tungri came from the Lower Rhine. The Thracians had their original home much further east, and the Hamii were first enrolled in Syria. Only one unit, the Cavalry Regiment of Tungri, was made up wholly of horsemen. Others were infantry units with a mounted contingent used as scouts, escorts or despatch riders. The fact that certain forts had more than one auxiliary unit attached to them seems to mean that the garrisons were changed at least once during the Antonine occupation.

It was not only in size that the known Antonine Wall forts differed from one another. They varied in their defences and in their shape. All but two were defended by ramparts of turf or clay. The two exceptions, Castlecary and Balmuildy, were enclosed by stone walls, doubtless because these two forts had a particularly important function to perform. Balmuildy certainly guarded a crossing of the River Kelvin, and it has been suggested that both forts were terminals of roads leading to the Wall from the south. The road running down the Clyde valley probably divided north of Carluke, one branch making for Castlecary and the other for Balmuildy.

Only a few of the excavated forts were exactly rectangular, the others being rather irregular quadrilaterals. Their ditch systems of course varied too, even from one side of a fort to another. The number and dimensions of the

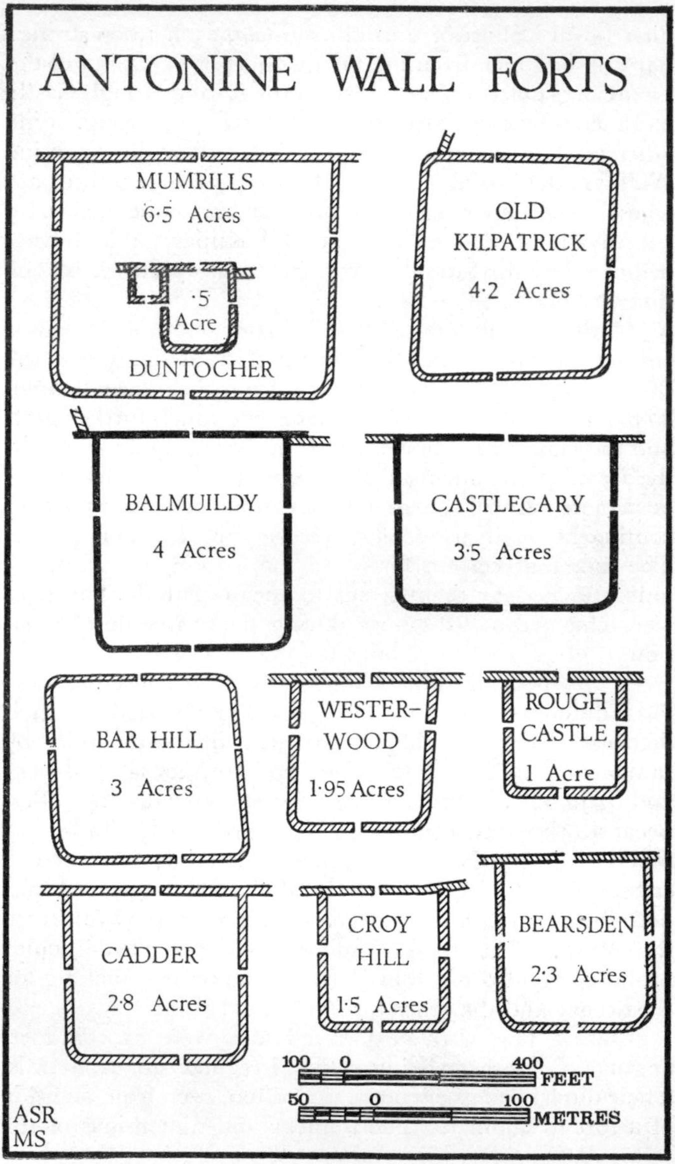

ANTONINE WALL FORTS

MUMRILLS
6·5 Acres

·5 Acre
DUNTOCHER

OLD KILPATRICK
4·2 Acres

BALMUILDY
4 Acres

CASTLECARY
3·5 Acres

BAR HILL
3 Acres

WESTER–WOOD
1·95 Acres

ROUGH CASTLE
1 Acre

CADDER
2·8 Acres

CROY HILL
1·5 Acres

BEARSDEN
2·3 Acres

100   0   400
FEET
50   0   100
METRES

ASR
MS

FIGURE 8

ditches were dictated by the strength or weakness of the ground in front.

The known Antonine Wall forts all had their free-standing corners rounded, and all had the usual four gates, one in each of the four sides, except for tiny Duntocher, which had no south gate, probably because the southern slope on which the fort stood was too steep to carry wheeled traffic. The fort gates were usually flanked by gate-towers, containing guard-chambers on the ground level, and upper storeys from which it was possible to gain access to the rampart walk on top of the fort walls. These walls would average about 10 feet (3 m.) in height, and like the Antonine Wall itself would probably be surmounted by wooden breastworks, or in the case of stone-walled forts by stone battlements. At the corners of the forts too there were often watch-towers.

All the excavated forts had principal buildings in the centre of the internal area, and most had barrack blocks in front of and behind the central block. In the case of very small forts, however, like Rough Castle and Duntocher, the " principal buildings " may have been no more than unit offices, most of the administrative work being conducted from a larger fort nearby.

The principal buildings were usually of stone, with heavy red-tiled roofs. In a large fort, these included the Headquarters Building (*principia*), containing one or two courtyards and a range of small rooms at the back, the central room of which was the shrine (*aedes* or *sacellum*); the Officers' Quarters (*praetorium*); and granaries distinguished by their buttressed walls strong enough to support massive roofs. Room had also to be found for workshops and stores. The barrack blocks in front of and behind the central block were usually of wood.

Each fort also had at least one suite of baths, situated either inside, or else just outside the fort defences within an annexe. The bath-house was not only a cleaning establishment, but was also a social centre. An altar to the goddess Fortuna (Good Luck) has often been found in a bath-house,

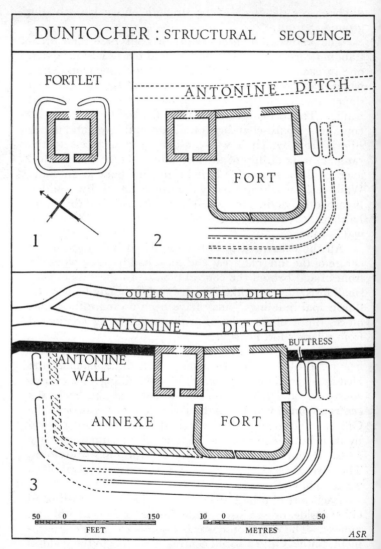

DUNTOCHER : STRUCTURAL SEQUENCE

FORTLET

ANTONINE DITCH

FORT

1

2

OUTER NORTH DITCH

ANTONINE DITCH

BUTTRESS

ANTONINE WALL

ANNEXE

FORT

3

50   0   150   10   0   50
            FEET   METRES

ASR

FIGURE 9

an indication perhaps that games of chance were played in its ante-rooms. An adequate water supply for drinking, washing and other purposes was provided either by wells (almost every Headquarters Building had a well in its courtyard), by rainwater cisterns or by aqueducts leading from nearby streams.

The forts on the Antonine Wall in its final form were separated by much shorter intervals than the 6 mile (10 km.) intervals between forts on Hadrian's Wall. On the Antonine Wall of course the enemy was so much closer, just across the isthmus valley and over the hills. It has long been known that in its final form Hadrian's Wall had sixteen forts, milecastles set at every Roman mile, and between each pair of milecastles two turrets or watch-towers. Until recently, however, it has been thought that there were no comparable minor structures on the Antonine Wall. Even the small Duntocher fortlet, about 60 feet (18 m.) square and so like a milecastle, did not seem exactly comparable, since it occurred at a site later occupied by a fort (Fig. 9).

Within recent decades, however, Professor J. K. S. St. Joseph has discovered from the air two enclosures attached to the back of the Antonine Wall, one in Wilderness Plantation, about midway between the forts at Balmuildy and Cadder, and one at Glasgow Bridge, about midway between Cadder and Kirkintilloch. These enclosures measured internally 60-70 feet (18-21 m.) and they were marked on east, west and south sides by ditches (Fig. 7).

These two enclosures were rather similar in dimensions to the so-called " guard-house " (found in 1894) at Watling Lodge, about midway between the forts at Rough Castle and Falkirk. The Watling Lodge guard-house stood at the point where the Roman road passed through the frontier northwards in the direction of the fort at Camelon, and this has long been regarded as a sufficient reason for its existence. The discovery of the two enclosures at Wilderness Plantation and at Glasgow Bridge suggested that even had there not been a road interrupting the line of the Antonine Wall at

Watling Lodge, there might still have been an enclosure or fortlet there.

At all three points, Watling Lodge, Glasgow Bridge and Wilderness Plantation, the Wall and Ditch changed direction quite distinctly, and the intervals between the forts on either side were rather longer than usual—well over 4,000 yards (3,600 m.). Until a few years ago, it was thought that this might be an adequate explanation for the presence of the fortlets, and the term " interval-fortlets " was suggested as an acceptable interim name.

It was suggested too that the most likely sites on which to seek for more " interval-fortlets " were in three other areas where there were unusually long intervals between forts, that is between Inveravon and Mumrills, between Balmuildy and Bearsden, and between Duntocher and Old Kilpatrick. A search at Polmont between Inveravon and Mumrills proved negative. There is no immediately obvious site on the very vulnerable stretch of the frontier between Duntocher and Old Kilpatrick, but on the striking eminence of Crow Hill, about a mile (1·6 km.) west of Balmuildy, the lines of the Antonine Wall and Ditch again changed direction, sharply. Here, it was thought, another " interval-fortlet " might await discovery, but a search for it in 1961 proved inconclusive.

In 1977, however, two new fortlets were found by excavation, one by Mr. W. S. Hanson about 250 feet (80 m.) west of the Antonine Wall fort on Croy Hill, and the other by Mr. L. J. F. Keppie and Mr. J. Walker just west of Seabegs Wood. Each measured internally about 73 feet (c. 22 m.) by 60-62 feet (18-18·8 m.). In 1978 Mr. Keppie and Mr. Walker found yet another fortlet at Kinneil, about 600 yards (540 m.) west of Kinneil House. It was much destroyed, but probably measured 60 feet (18 m.) across from east to west.

Seven fortlets have now been identified on the line of the Antonine Wall, at Kinneil, Watling Lodge, Seabegs, Croy Hill, Glasgow Bridge, Wilderness, and Duntocher. It was long ago suggested by Mr. J. Clarke that another fortlet may

once have stood on Castlehill, west of Bearsden (in addition
to the possible Peel Burn fortlet c. 500 yards (460 m.) west
of Castlehill, which was postulated by early antiquaries).
More recently, Mr. J. Gillam has suggested that another
fortlet may be disguised by the small enclosure outside the
east gate of the Antonine Wall fort at Rough Castle.

So far, however, only seven fortlets are known with
certainty along the 37-mile (c. 60 km.) length of the
Antonine Wall. Those at Kinneil, Seabegs, Croy Hill and
Wilderness seem to have been of contemporary build with
the Antonine Wall or its stone base, and the Watling Lodge
" guard-house " appears likely to have been so. The
Glasgow Bridge fortlet has not yet been excavated, and the
Duntocher fortlet stood alone for a time until a fort was
added to its east side before the Antonine Wall arrived.
(This is the strongest evidence for the belief that the
Antonine Wall was built from east to west.)

Two of the seven known fortlets were later replaced by
forts, that at Croy Hill by a fort east of the fortlet, that at
Duntocher by a fort on the same site. Three of the known
fortlets, at Watling Lodge, Glasgow Bridge and Wilderness
stood midway between pairs of forts. The sixth and seventh
known fortlets, at Kinneil and Seabegs, may be fairly near
expected but as yet undiscovered fort-sites. The Antonine
Ditch swept past the sites of all the known fortlets without a
break, as indeed it also swept, unbroken, past the forts at
Westerwood, Croy Hill (there being an 80 foot (25 m.) gap
to the east), Bar Hill, Bearsden and Duntocher. Stretches
of the Antonine Wall and Ditch were clearly not all
completed at one time.

With seven fortlets known, there is now growing evidence
for the construction of fortlets at frequent intervals, either
between pairs of forts, or as predecessors to forts.

Meanwhile, Mr. J. Gillam has suggested that the
Antonine Wall was *originally* intended to reproduce the
system developed on Hadrian's Wall, with large forts at
intervals of about every 6 miles (c. 10 km.), and milecastles
(or fortlets) at every Roman mile (and possibly two turrets

between each pair of fortlets). This system, he has further suggested, was later changed on the Antonine Wall to incorporate forts at 2-mile (3·2 km.) intervals.

It is the case that in the Antonine Wall frontier area six large forts were almost certainly constructed at an early stage, at intervals of 6-8 miles (10-13 km.) apart. These were at Carriden, Mumrills, Castlecary, Bar Hill, Balmuildy and Old Kilpatrick.

Castlecary and Balmuildy were defended by stone walls, and were probably terminals of land-routes from the south, carrying supplies. Each of these forts had squared north corners, in anticipation of the arrival of the Antonine Wall in due course, and the fort at Balmuildy even sent off little stone wings from its north corners to facilitate the junction of the Antonine Wall with the fort.

At Mumrills, the plan of the fort shows that it too sent off wings from its north corners, although this is not generally recognised. Its wings, continuing the north rampart of the fort, were 15 feet (4·5 m.) wide, like the Antonine Wall itself. Mumrills fort also performed a special function. It was the largest fort on the line, and, besides accommodating a regiment of cavalry, it probably held the headquarters staff of the Antonine Wall project.

The forts at Carriden, Bar Hill and Old Kilpatrick each had all four corners rounded, and presumably stood alone for a time. Carriden and Old Kilpatrick commanded the waterways of the Forth and Clyde respectively, and protected seaborne supplies. Bar Hill, lying c. 495 feet (c. 150 m.) above sea-level, was one of the highest points on the line, and in Roman times had a panoramic outlook along the line, and across the isthmus valley to the Kilsyth and Campsie Hills, with their ever-present threat to Roman activity.

These six forts, then, at Carriden, Mumrills, Castlecary, Bar Hill, Balmuildy and Old Kilpatrick, made an early appearance in the Antonine Wall frontier area. They were also, as far as is at present known, the largest forts on the frontier. At least four out of seven known fortlets were also early, being of one build with the Antonine Wall or its stone base. Two fortlets, at Croy Hill and Duntocher, were later replaced by forts which were smaller than the large early forts. This establishes a sequence of events, but does not prove, beyond doubt, *an original intention* that the Antonine Wall should never have more than six large forts, with fortlets at every Roman mile.

On the contrary, one of the smallest Antonine Wall forts, at Rough Castle, had an uninterrupted gap for a causeway in the Antonine Ditch exactly opposite the fort's north gateway, and not opposite a putative fortlet to the east. This small fort came into existence early, too, or at least before the Antonine Ditch was completed in this area. Much still remains to be learned about the constructional sequence of all elements of the Antonine frontier.

The tale of known structures attached to the Antonine Wall is not yet complete. At certain points on the line small turf platforms were built against the back of the Wall. These, it was suggested by Sir George Macdonald, were for use in signalling (Fig. 7).

Six of these platforms have long been known. They occur in three pairs, one pair to east and one to west of the fort at Rough Castle, and another pair on the western slope of Croy Hill. The excavation, by Dr. K. A. Steer, of the platform immediately west of the fort at Rough Castle, has shown it to have been 17 feet (5 m.) square and formed of turf set on a stone base. The turf was bonded into the Antonine Wall, but sealed a gravel pit dug for the construction of the Military Way which must therefore at this point have preceded the erection of the turf superstructure of the platform and of the Antonine Wall. Evidence of burning confirmed the view that on this platform (and others like it) there had stood signalling beacons. Dr. Steer has suggested that the two pairs of platforms on either side of Rough Castle may have been intended for signalling northwards and the Croy Hill pair for signalling southwards.

In 1977, the Royal Commission on Ancient and Historical Monuments (Scotland) located or discovered on air photographs three sub-rectangular ditched enclosures apparently attached to the rear of the Antonine Wall in Wilderness Plantation (Fig. 7). There were two about 260 yards (230 m.) on either side of the Wilderness fortlet, and a third about 330 yards (300 m.) to the west. They seem to have measured about 40 by 26 feet (c. 12 by 8 m.). Their purpose is not yet known.

The Antonine Wall crossed several small streams in its course from Forth to Clyde, for example the Rowan Tree Burn at Rough Castle, but the Rivers Avon and Kelvin were the only rivers of considerable size which had to be negotiated. On approaching the River Avon the Wall and Ditch reached the east bank at a point much lower downstream than that at which they left the river on its west bank. Sir George Macdonald suggested that the intention was to leave space for a small fort on the east bank. In 1967 a small Roman structure (possibly a small fort) was in fact found there.

At Balmuildy, on the other hand, where the line of the Wall crossed the River Kelvin, remains of stone abutments, stone piers, and possibly of the wooden superstructure of a bridge have been dredged up from the river bed to the north of the site of the fort, and about 90 yards (c. 82 m.) from its north-west corner. Their position as they were dredged up was carefully noted and was such as to suggest that the bridge had continued the line of the Military Way across the river, rather than the line of the Wall. In that case the ends of the Wall and Ditch on each side of the river must have been retained in some way and the rampart walk on top of the Wall must have been linked with the Military Way by paths or tracks. The Military Way must here have approached very close to the Wall, the interval between the two being about 10 yards (9 m.) instead of the usual 40-50 yards (36-46 m.). The reason would be, in the words of Mr. S. N. Miller, " to secure that the bridge with its parapet should provide a barrier to fill the gap in the Wall, while the Military Way, in this position, could take the place of the rampart walk of the Wall for patrolling purposes ".

There may also have been obstacles to bar passage under the bridge between the piers (Fig. 19).

It has been suggested that the stone-walled fort at Balmuildy was one of the terminals of a road running down Clydesdale. In that case, the Military Way at Balmuildy would receive traffic from the south as well as from east and west. It is possible that here too native traffic may have been permitted to cross the Roman frontier. If so, it would certainly be under the scrutiny of guards on the fort walls, and may even have had to pass through a guard-house or checkpoint at a passage through the Wall on the north bank of the Kelvin.

The Antonine frontier line could still not have been regarded as complete until provision had been made to guard against enemy landings on the south banks of the Forth and Clyde. The danger was lessened on the Forth by the existence of a Roman road running along its south bank from Inveresk through Cramond, where there was a harbour, to the fort at Carriden. From Carriden the road would run north-west for about three-quarters of a mile (1·2 km.) to join the Military Way.

At the more vulnerable west end of the Wall the Romans displayed their usual acute and energetic grasp of local conditions. A Roman road ran westwards from the terminal fort at Old Kilpatrick, probably to a base established for the reception of supplies at a point on the Clyde below Old Kilpatrick, possibly at Dumbarton. This was the highest point to which in Roman times the Clyde was navigable for any but the smallest craft. Indeed, at Dumbuck, between Old Kilpatrick and Dumbarton, the river could actually be forded at low tide.

A base on the Clyde below Dumbarton might also have accommodated a small naval squadron, charged with the task of keeping the Firth free of enemy craft. Attempts by North Britons to land on the south bank of the Clyde were also anticipated and provided against by the construction of a fort at Whitemoss, Bishopton, overlooking the ford at Dumbuck and just over 2 miles (3·2 km.) as the crow flies from Old Kilpatrick, and of a fortlet, 8 miles (13 km.) to the west, on Lurg Moor, above Greenock. In 1970 Mr. F. Newall discovered another fortlet at Outerwards, above Largs, 6 miles (10 km.) south-west of Lurg Moor.

Our knowledge of the Antonine frontier is no doubt still far from complete. Many new discoveries have been made during recent decades, and there are probably many more yet to come. Its general appearance in Roman times is, however, not in doubt.

A North Briton who made his way south through a gap like the Blane Valley gap and looked towards the southern scarp of the isthmus valley would see, running east and west for mile after mile, the great barrier of the Wall itself, towering up, probably with a wooden breastwork, to a height not far short of 20 feet (6 m.), and the deep ravine of the Ditch in front. His eye would pick out the forts, with their high turf ramparts or battlemented stone walls, their forbidding gateways and watch-towers, and the red-tiled roofs of the main fort-buildings. Between forts, along the rampart walk on top of the Wall, patrols carried out their ceaseless vigil. As his gaze strained hopefully, or despairingly, westwards beyond the end of the Wall itself, there would come into view the Roman supply base on the Clyde, busy with small Roman craft, and the Roman stations continuing along the south bank of the Clyde from Bishopton to Lurg Moor and far beyond. Even a distant view of the great frontier would impress—was intended to impress— the native beholder with a sense of his own helplessness against the power and majesty of Rome.

Protected by the Wall, and concealed from a watcher to the north, there ran the Military Way, which, besides carrying east-west traffic, was linked to and supported by the elaborate system of roads, forts, and fortlets, which covered South Scotland and even penetrated far into Perthshire. Over the people of Dumfriesshire in particular there was clamped down a grid of roads, widely-spaced forts and close-set fortlets or watch-posts. The Romans clearly had information about a threat to peace from this area in the

Antonine period which is not yet in the hands of the modern archaeologist (Fig. 2).

It may be reckoned that a force approaching 20,000 men might have been needed to garrison the forts on the Antonine Wall and the twenty or more Antonine forts and fortlets elsewhere in Scotland. Whence did they come?

The forts on Hadrian's Wall were not, it seems, abandoned when the Antonine Wall was built, but their auxiliary garrisons may have been replaced by small caretaker units of legionary troops. Even if there were not proof of the replacement of auxiliaries by legionaries for this purpose, it would still be reasonable to suppose that when the Antonine Wall was built, part if not all of the auxiliary garrison force on Hadrian's Wall could be released for garrison duty farther north. Even, however, if there were evidence that the entire auxiliary force from the forts on Hadrian's Wall— reckoned as about 12,000 men—was sent north for this purpose, it would not have sufficed to provide garrisons for even the known Antonine forts in Scotland. Garrisons would still have had to be sought from other sources.

One other source of supply for the Antonine garrison force in Scotland was apparently the north of England, between Derby and the Tyne. Several forts in that area (with the exception of those on the Cumberland coast) seem to have been deprived of their garrisons in the early Antonine period.

Another source of supply for Antonine Wall garrisons, it was long ago suggested by Sir George Macdonald, may have been the legionary force in Britain, contrary though it was to normal Roman practice to use legionary troops as frontier garrisons. Certainly inscriptions show that legionaries built several of the Antonine Wall forts, that legionaries were buried between the forts at Bar Hill and Auchendavy, and that legionaries dedicated altars to favourite deities while operating in some capacity on the Antonine Wall. There is definite proof too that for a time a detachment of the Twentieth Legion formed part of the garrison of at least one of the forts in South Scotland, the most important fort on the eastern route, at Newstead on the Tweed.

Whatever the character and source of the garrison force sent north to hold the Antonine forts and fortlets in Scotland, either on or off the Wall, there is no doubt that it was superlatively well equipped and supplied. The " small finds " or movable objects recovered, through excavation or by chance discovery, from Antonine sites in Scotland, and now preserved mainly in the National Museum of Antiquities, Edinburgh, or in the Hunterian Museum, Glasgow University, illustrate the thoroughness of the Roman army supply system, and the skill and versatility of the Roman army craftsmen.

There are examples of competent, and even fine mason's work, like the columns and capitals which once graced the courtyard of the Headquarters Building at Bar Hill; squared building stones with ornamental tooling on their outer faces; and stones grooved with channels to carry water-pipes. Careful woodworking is exemplified in well-shaped beams and posts, wheels, buckets, pulleys, etc.

There survive, too, lengths of clay water-pipes, jointed to fit the next length, and clay tiles for various purposes. Flanged tiles and semi-cylindrical tiles were used in tiling roofs. Box tiles, or flue tiles were used to construct flues in the walls of a room which was to be heated by the hypocaust method of central heating. The floor of such a room was supported on pillars formed of square flat tiles set one on top of the other. The air in the pillared basement or hypocaust was heated from a furnace outside, and the hot air was led upwards through flues concealed in the walls of the room above and covered with wall plaster.

Coal, as well as wood, was used for heating hypocaust furnaces and for smelting ores. British iron ores, and native deposits of lead and copper, supplied the military smith with material for the upkeep of the arms, armour and everyday tools required by the men of his unit, for the harness of any horses attached to it, as well as for more specialised implements and fittings.

36

Many articles of leather too have been recovered from Antonine forts. It is known that one form of tribute exacted by the Romans from subject peoples was the provision of hides. Large numbers of skins were required by Roman army tanners to manufacture into waterproof leather tents (for use in campaigning or on manoeuvres), jerkins, breeches, knapsacks, shoes, etc.

It was mainly from the great store-depots in the north of England and even further south that the Roman army of North Britain drew its supplies of tiles, window-glass, ores and some manufactured articles of metal, and possibly leather goods, as well as a variety of vessels and other equipment for use in the storing, preparing, cooking and eating of food. These included rotary querns or mill-stones for grinding corn, stone mortars, stone troughs, stone and lead weights, wooden barrels, bronze cooking pots, glass bottles, coarse clay store-jars, clay cooking pots, bowls, jugs, beakers, lamps, etc., and the fine red highly-glossed table ware known as samian ware. This was imported into Britain from the continent, and seems to have been greatly prized by its owners. Many samian plates and cups have the owner's name or mark scratched on them.

Part, at least, of the food supply of the Roman army in North Britain came from store-depots in the south. Some grain was thus supplied and was stored in the massive stone granaries near the centre of each fort. Agricultural implements, like the famous scythes from Newstead, do, however, suggest that at times the Roman garrison force in Scotland may have supplemented its official issue of grain with home produced crops. The other staple items of Roman military diet—milk, cheese and meat—were doubtless also acquired locally. Oil, wine and a few other delicacies would, however, have been imported from the continent.

The provisioning and maintenance of the Roman army of North Britain must have depended both on sea-borne traffic to harbours on the Forth and Clyde, and on an efficient and regular system of land-transport, as well as on ample storage accommodation in the frontier areas. The Roman roads leading north to the Antonine Wall, and the Military Way behind the Wall, must have carried a constant stream of Roman wagons, no less constant perhaps than the stream of long-distance lorries on our modern trunk roads. Overnight accommodation and parking places for wagons would be offered by the road-posts or fortlets in South Scotland, and stores for their contents must have been provided at every Roman fort of any size. Store-houses would stand conveniently in or near the central block of principal buildings, as did the granaries. Nearby too were usually placed the military workshops, close to the stored material.

Wagons, however, could be allowed to stand outside a fort, except when actually unloading at a granary or store-house, and their transient drivers could even be lodged close to their vehicles. In fact, many (if not all) of the Antonine forts in Scotland, both on and off the Wall, had annexes attached to them, enclosed by ramparts and ditches of slighter character than the fort defences. A bath-house, too, it will be remembered, often stood outside a fort, within an annexe.

Whatever their original purpose, however, fort annexes seem in time to have accommodated more than Roman wagons, their drivers, and bath-houses. The tombstones from the Roman cemetery between the Antonine Wall forts at Bar Hill and Auchendavy included one which bore the name of a lady, Verecunda, and a second which was set up by a father Salmanes over his fifteen-year-old son Salmanes. Salmanes senior, whose name was apparently of Semitic origin, may it is thought have been an eastern trader. In any case, Verecunda and fifteen-year-old Salmanes were uncompromisingly civilian. Verecunda might perhaps be regarded as the wife of a fort-commander, in the event of his being allowed to have his wife with him, but Salmanes could hardly have been the son of a Roman officer or soldier.

From other Antonine fort-sites too, notably Balmuildy and Bar Hill, have come objects which betray the presence of women and children, in no small numbers. From Bar Hill alone have come far more women's and children's shoes (in a great variety of sizes) than could reasonably be assigned to the (hypothetical) family of a fort-commander.

The most striking evidence, however, for the growth of a civilian settlement alongside a fort came with the 1956 discovery at Carriden of an altar set up to the god Jove by the community of villagers settled at the fort Velunia or Velunias (that is Carriden), the matter being arranged for them by a certain Aelius Mansuetus. The settlers outside this fort had attained the official status of a *vicus*—a village community as had no doubt others on the Antonine frontier and at other Antonine sites in Scotland.

The Latin names of Aelius Mansuetus and Verecunda, and the eastern name of Salmanes need not mean that all civilians in Roman fort-annexes were Roman, or of Mediterranean origin. There would also be native Britons, come to trade or to settle, or, in the case of women, to marry Roman soldiers and to bring up children. There were certainly many contacts between Roman and native both in and beyond occupied or protected territory as a result of which much Roman material—particularly Roman coins and pottery—found its way into native possession, either by legitimate or by illegitimate means. They cannot all be explained as souvenirs or curios collected from long-deserted Roman forts and then lost again on distant native sites.

Friendly contact, however, between Roman and native appears to have been largely restricted to the southern lowlands of Scotland, to occupied territory. Most of the North Britons to the north of the Antonine Wall seem to have been obstinately hostile, as were also perhaps the natives of the extreme south-west, particularly in Dumfriesshire.

Excavation has shown that Antonine forts in Scotland were destroyed, at least once (and at certain sites on the Antonine Wall itself, possibly twice), and were again reoccupied by the Romans, often with changed garrisons and alterations in fort-plans, before being finally abandoned. The date of the final abandonment is still a matter of controversy. It may be that the Antonine Wall itself, and the Antonine system generally, were gradually run down, while Hadrian's Wall was gradually rehabilitated as the frontier. This would explain discrepancies between the dates in the A.D. 160s assigned by pottery specialists to the latest known pottery from certain Antonine Wall forts, and the evidence of later second-century coins (both from hoards and site-finds) from some sites on the Antonine Wall and elsewhere in Scotland, combined with, for example, an inscription at Castlecary of the period A.D. 175-190, and later second-century pottery at, for example, Mumrills, Castlecary, Birrens, and Newstead.

It was for no more than a few decades then, that the Antonine Wall formed the most north-westerly frontier of the Roman Empire. During that period, the Wall served as a base for military operations into enemy territory, with a line of outpost forts running to the gate of the Scottish Highlands. It also formed a physical and psychological barrier separating the tribes north of the Forth-Clyde line from Roman-protected territory to the south. Indeed, the whole Antonine system in Scotland was designed to break up and to isolate disaffected elements and to exercise a watchful control over the movements of natives north and south of the Wall. Many of the Antonine Wall forts had strong defences to south, and some South Scottish forts even faced south. Although the full details of this scheme are only gradually coming to light, yet enough is already known to command admiration for this " colossal undertaking " which guaranteed security for a generation to the civilian areas in Roman Britain.

The life of the Antonine Wall did not of course stop short with its evacuation by the Romans before the end of the 2nd century A.D. " For the Antonine Wall and other Roman works did not sink silently into the ground when the Roman occupation finally ended, like stage sets gliding aside or upwards when one act gives place to another. They still stood through succeeding centuries ". Every ancient structure of any permanence belongs not only to its own age, but to every age which comes after.

The elaborate Roman road system continued to offer convenient routes to post-Roman travellers. The massive Roman forts and other Roman works remained a familiar feature of the post-Roman landscape, and provided later visitors with shelter and even with unexpected windfalls of Roman material. The Antonine Wall and Ditch withstood obliteration century after century, serving if not as a barrier, at least as a boundary, a march or else as a trysting-place. They are a trysting-place still to pilgrims on the track of their surviving remains.

THE REMAINS OF THE ANTONINE FRONTIER

The modern pilgrims who follow the line of the Antonine Wall will be walking in the footsteps not only of the Romans but also of many earlier antiquaries, who walked or occasionally rode along its line. Walking is still by far the best method of traversing any part of the course of the Wall, and indeed certain stretches of it can only be reached by walking a short distance from the nearest road. Those unable or disinclined to walk far will, however, find that they can drive by car to many points upon the line from which they may enjoy a fine impression of the remains and a magnificent prospect.

Whatever the means of locomotion, Antonine Wall pilgrims will encounter no such dangers as awaited visitors to Hadrian's Wall in the seventeenth and eighteenth centuries, when the Roman forts on the southern Wall were used as dens by Border robbers. They will remember, however, that should they leave a public road to walk through private ground or fields, a courteous and considerately-timed request for the owner's permission to do so will smooth the path.

The Antonine Wall was almost certainly built from east

to west. It is usually found convenient to describe the remains from east to west and to follow that direction on the ground. " The remains " usually mean in fact the Antonine Ditch, for the Wall has not survived the centuries so well, and can seldom be traced for any great distance at a time. The Military Way, being laid on the surface, has suffered most, and rarely can its line be detected. The defences of some of the Antonine Wall forts can, however, still be seen.

The description which follows deals very briefly with those parts of the line where the remains are not clearly visible, and lingers over well-preserved features. The whole line is shown on the endpaper map. Reference should also be made to the Ordnance Survey $2\frac{1}{2}$ in. map of the Antonine Wall, first published in 1969.

Bridgeness to Kinneil

If there was ever a fort on the Wall at Bridgeness itself, its position is now unknown. Its place may have been taken by the fort at Carriden, about $\frac{3}{4}$-mile (1·2 km.) south-east of the end of the Wall, and in that case there may have been a fortlet at Bridgeness, its vestiges now buried beneath the town of Bo'ness.

The fort at Carriden was discovered through aerial survey in 1945 by Professor St. Joseph in the policies of Carriden House on a shelf about 100 feet (30 m.) above sea-level. Its existence, however, had long been regarded as very probable, on the evidence of " Roman Altars, Inscriptions, and Coins . . . dug up at this Place ", as recorded by Alexander Gordon.

Professor St. Joseph's air photographs indicate that the fort measured about 400 feet (120 m.) from north to south, and at least 400 feet (120 m.) from west to east. It had three ditches on its east and south-east sides. The position of its east gate suggests that it faced south. Trial trenching and accidental discovery have brought to light some Antonine pottery.

In 1956 a Roman altar was ploughed up about 150 yards (140 m.) to the east of the fort. The inscription on it is of twofold importance. In the first place, it establishes the presence beside the fort at Carriden of *vicani*—people of the *vicus* or officially recognised village community. Secondly it gives the Roman name of the fort at Carriden as Velunia(s). This shows that the list of " cities " in the narrowest part of Britain, that is on the Forth-Clyde isthmus, which is given in the seventh-century Ravenna " Cosmography ", ran from east to west. The list reads:— Velunia, Volitanio, Pexa, Begesse, Colanica, Medio-nemeton, Subdobiadon, Litana, Cibra, Credigone. Apart from Velunia(s), it is uncertain which of these names should be assigned to which Antonine Wall forts.

In Roman times there would be an uninterrupted view from the fort at Carriden to the end of the Wall, $\frac{3}{4}$-mile (1·2 km.) to the north-west at Bridgeness. Between the two the Forth itself would serve as the frontier, with the Roman road from Cramond running along the south bank of the estuary until it joined the Military Way behind the Wall.

The east end of the Antonine Wall was probably very close to where ruinous Bridgeness Tower now stands, on a rocky knoll which in Roman times, as Sir George Mac-donald observed, was probably " a little headland, project-ing into the Firth, with bays sweeping back behind it on the east and on the west ". Alterations in the coast-line since Roman times have now left it high and dry.

The legionary tablet set up at the east end of the Wall by men of the Second Legion to record the completion of 4,652 paces was found in 1868, just below Bridgeness Tower. The slab is now in the National Museum of Antiquities, Edinburgh, but the approximate place of discovery is marked by a modern tablet reproducing the inscription of the original slab, and set into the wall on the west side of Harbour Road below Bridgeness Tower.

The most easterly 2 miles (3·2 km.) of the Antonine Wall are obliterated by the modern town of Bo'ness, so that

43

no surface traces now remain. Its line is, however, preserved by a lane and a road bearing the significant names of Grahamsdyke Lane and Grahamsdyke Road respectively. Grahamsdyke or " Grymisdyke " was a name applied to the Antonine Wall as early as the fourteenth century. The fourteenth-century chronicler, John of Fordun, says it was so called because it was destroyed by a native British hero, Gryme. In the form Grahamsdyke the name has clung to the Antonine Wall until quite recent times.

Grahamsdyke Lane rises fairly rapidly to the level of the old 100-foot (30 m.) raised beach, and appears to overlie the Antonine Ditch. Grahamsdyke Road, too, and its continuation westwards—Dean Road—are laid partly over the Ditch. The Wall and Ditch here stood about 200 feet (60 m.) above sea-level. To the north there was a commanding outlook over the Firth of Forth towards the hills of Fife on the east and the mountains of Stirlingshire and Perthshire on the west.

The line then descended gradually to a point almost 2 miles (3·2 km.) from Bridgeness Tower, where Dean Road turns sharply north-westwards, at the former site of Dean House, while the Antonine Wall and Ditch ran straight on. From the public road a little way beyond its north-westerly turn, an avenue leads into Kinneil Estate, now a public park. The avenue through the park lies about 30 or 40 yards (27-36 m.) to the north of the Antonine Ditch, and a glance southwards from the avenue along the Dean or Gil Burn should reveal the most easterly surviving trace of the Ditch to be seen above ground. This is marked by a decided dip in the bank on the west side of the Dean or Gil Burn.

Kinneil to Inveravon

A fort would be expected at or near Kinneil House. No surface traces of it now survive, although the eighteenth-century antiquaries John Horsley and William Maitland refer to the remains of a fort. Sir George Macdonald suggested that it may rather have stood on the site of Dean House, on the east side of the Dean or Gil Burn, but excavation there in 1960 revealed no sign of a fort, although the Antonine Ditch was found. Farther west, in 1961, the Antonine Wall base and Ditch were located.

At Kinneil House itself, the line of the Wall and Ditch lay very close to the south gable of the house. They then crossed a rivulet to run westwards through a park known as " The Meadows " where the course of the Ditch can still be detected. Trenching by Sir George Macdonald within the Meadows revealed remains both of the Antonine Wall base and of the Military Way. In 1978, Mr. L. J. F. Keppie and Mr. J. Walker discovered the remains of a fortlet about 600 yards (540 m.) west of Kinneil House. It was of one build with the Antonine Wall.

After passing through the Meadows and a plantation to the west of it the Roman line reached the top of a slope descending steeply to the Firth and now known as the Cowbank. It may be conveniently reached from a minor road connecting Bo'ness and Polmont via Nether Kinneil and Inveravon. A path leads upwards from this road near an old quarry on to the top of the Cowbank. Here the Ditch is no longer visible, but the stone base of the Wall was discovered to the south of it in 1915.

West of the Cowbank, the line of the Ditch may be faintly seen turning south-west to climb a slope called the Summerhouse Park. Excavation there in 1961 established the line of Wall and Ditch. Now for the first time the Roman line begins to turn slightly away from the Firth in order to reach a range of low hills bordering the southern edge of the Carse of Falkirk.

A gap in the hedge on the west side of Summerhouse Park faces on to a hilly road aptly named " The Stey Step ", and exactly opposite the gap the Stey Step is joined at right angles by a road which runs westwards to Inveravon and Polmont. This road has been laid in the Ditch for much of the way from the Stey Step to Inveravon. The stone base of the Wall and remains of the Military Way have been detected in the fields to the south of the road. For much of the distance to Inveravon the line is at about 200 feet (60 m.) above sea-level.

Just to the east of Inveravon Cottages the modern road swings to the south of the Antonine frontier to pass Inveravon Farm and Inveravon Tower. In 1976 the Ditch was located at about 330 yards (300 m.) east of Inveravon Farm. To the west of Inveravon Tower the modern road emerges from a patch of trees to provide a wide, and at times breathtaking view downhill over the Carse of Falkirk, with the River Avon on the west winding northwards across the Roman frontier line towards the Firth of Forth.

INVERAVON TO MUMRILLS

From the modern road the ground slopes down to the River Avon, to rise again from its west bank to the plateau on which stood Polmonthill Farm. Between the river and the hill-top is the best preserved stretch of the Antonine Ditch so far encountered. Dr. John Buchanan's description of a century ago is still true today:—" It has the appearance of an immense slice cut out of the breast of the brae, with well-preserved edges ". A ski-slope now runs parallel to it on the south side.

A closer view of this stretch of the Ditch is best obtained by following the modern road north from Inveravon Tower, until it joins a road running west (B904). This westward road leads to a bridge over the River Avon, and from the bridge another road turns sharply east to run along the west bank of the Avon towards Polmonthill.

Considerations of spacing suggest that a fort should be found at or near Inveravon, and the earlier antiquaries do in fact record a tradition of its existence. Sir George Macdonald presented strong grounds for supposing that a fort stood on the gentle slope of the east bank of the River Avon. Trenching in this area over 60 years ago revealed traces of occupation and at least one potsherd which appeared to be of Antonine date. The trenching showed too that the Antonine Wall and Ditch seemed to reach the east bank of the Avon at a rather lower point downstream than that at which they left the west bank, as if to leave space for a small fort. In 1967 the line of the Antonine Wall was traced across the field on the east bank of the Avon and a small Roman structure was located 200-300 feet (60-90 m.) from the river bank. The structure had been attached to the rear of the Antonine Wall, and measured at least 90 feet (27 m.) from north to south and at least 100 feet (30 m.) from east to west. Much coarse ware pottery, of Antonine date, was found. In 1976 the Antonine Ditch was seen in section, and in 1973 members of the Scottish Sub-Aqua Club recorded a concentration of worked stones in the bed of the River Avon where the Antonine Wall ran down to its east bank.

To the west of Polmonthill, the Antonine frontier attained a fairly flat ridge, once again close on 200 feet (60 m.) above sea-level. This ridge is now occupied by Grangemouth Golf Course. It may be reached either from Polmonthill or from a rough path which climbs rapidly from the modern road (Inveravon to Polmont) towards a reservoir. Trenching by Sir George Macdonald on Polmonthill revealed the Wall base.

A stretch of the Ditch west of the reservoir has had its north bank levelled and the material from it pushed into the hollow, so that the Ditch now appears as a flattish terrace with a well-defined bank on its south side. West of this terrace, the line becomes obscured by thickly-growing Millhall Wood, by a stream, by a road running from north to south past Polmont Church to join the main road through Polmont from Linlithgow to Falkirk (A9), and by a new motorway from Edinburgh to Stirling (M9).

There is evidence that the Wall and Ditch ran to the north of the modern church of Polmont, and indeed just to the north of the ruins of the old church of Polmont. The Roman line west of Polmont cemetery has been cut through by the new motorway. Excavation there in 1960 revealed the stone base of the Wall.

47

In the field south of the motorway, between the Polmont Burn and the Westquarter Burn, apparent remains of the Military Way have been found. Further west, to the west of the Westquarter Burn, the Roman line is overlaid by the former village of Beancross. Excavation by Sir George Macdonald in 1915 revealed the Wall base. In 1973, trenching just to the south of Beancross located remains of the Wall base and Ditch.

Mumrills to Falkirk (Fig. 10)

Between Beancross and Mumrills farmhouse, the Antonine Wall and Ditch turn sharply south-west to meet the northern defences of the largest known fort on the Antonine Wall. Mumrills fort had an internal area of 6·5 acres (2·6 h.) and stood on an escarpment about 100 feet (30 m.) above sea-level, with a fairly steep slope to south and east. Its site now lies between the secondary Polmont-Beancross-Falkirk road (B904) and the major Polmont to Falkirk road (A9). These two roads are linked by a lane, the old Sandy Loan, which cuts through the fort near its west side.

No trace of the fort defences are now visible above ground. Excavations conducted by Sir George Macdonald in 1923-1928 have shown that the builders of the Antonine Wall and the fort-builders appear to have been working with knowledge of each other's plans. The Wall certainly seems to have accommodated itself to a site already selected for a fort. Its north rampart, already built and with little wings sent off from its north corners, was 15 feet (4·5 m.) wide, like the Antonine Wall itself, and the Ditch was 24 feet (7·2 m.) wide, with a gap at the north gate. The rampart on the other three sides of the fort was 12·5-13 feet (c. 3·9 m.) wide at the base, and there were two ditches on the east side, one on the south side, three on the north half of the west front, and four on the south half of that front.

Remains were found of the central range of stone buildings—Headquarters Building, two granaries and

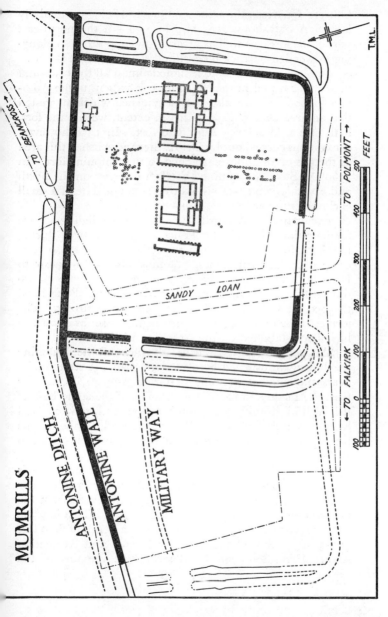

FIGURE 10

Officers' Quarters, the Officers' Quarters being particularly large. A bath-house was also located—in the north-east part of the fort—as well as several rows of postholes belonging to wooden barrack blocks, and the remains of streets.

Sir George Macdonald assigned almost all the coins and pottery recovered in the Mumrills excavations to the Antonine period, but he also found evidence which suggested that an area over 5 acres (2 h.) in extent, west of the fort, had once held a large Agricolan fort. In 1958 however, excavations carried out by Dr. K. Steer established this area as the site of an annexe attached to the Antonine fort. In 1960 Dr. Steer re-examined the fort defences on the north and east sides, and established the Antonine date of a small enclosure 120 yards (c. 110 m.) east of the fort.

Excavations at Mumrills have brought to light evidence for alterations in plan at least once and perhaps twice during the Antonine period. From the neighbourhood also have come two inscribed stones, a tombstone and an altar to Hercules Magusanus, recording the presence there of two different auxiliary units, a Cavalry Regiment of Tungri and the Second Cohort of Thracians, each 500 strong. The former is the only purely cavalry regiment so far known to have been stationed on the Antonine Wall.

Westwards from Mumrills, the line of the Antonine Ditch is again usurped by a modern road. A stretch of it bears the significant name of Grahamsdyke Street. Sir George Macdonald found the remains of the stone base of the Wall in ground to the south of the road, now covered by houses and gardens. At its western end, Grahamsdyke Street slopes down to join the main road from Polmont to Falkirk (A9).

Just to the west of the junction, the Roman line is crossed by the main road, to emerge on its south side. For a stretch of about half a mile (·8 km.) westward from the private grounds of Callendar Park College of Education, the Ditch survives in very fine condition to a depth of 6-10 feet (1·8-3 m.) within Callendar Park Leisure and Recreation Area. Here, too, can be detected the remains of the

50

Antonine Wall itself, in the form of a low mound running parallel to the Ditch on its south side, and here, too, can be seen the outer mound on the north side.

FALKIRK TO ROUGH CASTLE

The growth of modern Falkirk has now obliterated the line of the Wall and Ditch between Callendar Park on its east side and the district named Arnothill on its west side. Trenching by Sir George Macdonald did, however, locate the Wall base. The only relics of a possible fort which have been recorded are Roman potsherds and at least one Roman coin.

The line of the Wall on the west side of Falkirk is best reached by turning off the main Glasgow-Falkirk road (A9) up a fairly steep side road bearing the name of Arnothill. At the top of the ascent, Arnothill is joined at right angles by a lane running westwards—Arnothill Lane—which lies just over the north edge of the Ditch. The hollow of the Ditch is still visible inside the boundary fence of " Mayfield " (now the offices of Barratt Developments (Falkirk)). It stands at the west end of Arnothill Lane, here crossed at right angles by the enchantingly named " Maggie Wood's Loan ".

The Antonine frontier runs under Maggie Wood's Loan to enter the former lands of Bantaskine. These have recently been developed for housing by private builders but the position of the Antonine frontier is marked by a line of beech trees. At the west end of this line, a stretch of the Ditch was cleared out many years ago, and, though now thickly tree-grown, remains a formidable obstacle. Part of the counterscarp or north bank of the Ditch has been cut down or terraced to accommodate a modern track. To the west, during the construction of Falkirk's southern link road, Mr. L. J. F. Keppie uncovered a stretch of 150 feet (45 m.) of the Antonine Wall base (with three culverts), and examined the Antonine Ditch, just north of Falkirk High School. Between the western boundary wall of Falkirk

High School and the former " Lock Sixteen " on the Forth-Clyde Canal the line is obscured by housing developments and by construction works connected with the Canal.

West of " Lock Sixteen ", the Ditch appears in its finest condition anywhere along the whole line. This remarkable stretch of Ditch may be reached from the east by turning south along the canal bank, or from the west by turning southwards off the main Falkirk-Glasgow road to follow the secondary road to High Bonnybridge (B816). Just after the High Bonnybridge road has passed over the canal it twice turns sharply westwards, and from this point (Tamfourhill Road) the Antonine Ditch runs parallel to the road on its south side for about $\frac{1}{4}$-mile ($\cdot$4 km.). The Ditch here is about 40 feet wide (12 m.) and 15 feet (4$\cdot$5 m.) deep. In 1961, the stone base of the Wall was found.

A walker who proceeds along the bottom of the Ditch will have a vivid impression of the formidable nature of this obstacle as he sees the sides towering above him. If, again, he follows the path along the north edge of the Ditch, he may gaze down into the trough of the Ditch, or if he turns northwards and westwards, he will see the Kilsyth Hills looming into view across the plain immediately to the north.

This stretch of the Ditch ends at the villa called Watling Lodge. Here, in 1972, excavation by Dr. D. J. Breeze determined the size of a fortlet, attached to the rear of the wall at this point where it changed direction, and where the Roman road from the south passed through the frontier in the direction of the fort at Camelon ($\frac{3}{4}$-mile (1$\cdot$2 km.) to the north) and beyond. The fortlet measured, inside its rampart, over 60 feet (18$\cdot$5 m.) from east to west and over 50 feet (15$\cdot$5 m.) from north to south.

About 200 yards (180 m.) west of Watling Lodge, the hollow of the Ditch may be seen on the south side of the road (Falkirk to High Bonnybridge), and a little farther west, as the road inclines southwards, the hollow appears on its north side behind a brick wall. Here in 1973 remains of the Wall base were uncovered. As the road straightens out again, it once more runs parallel to the line of the Wall and

Ditch, on their south side, and it may even lie over the Military Way. In the garden of one of the private houses on the north side of the road—" Tayavalla "—a wooden bridge has been thrown over the Ditch, here close upon 10 feet (3 m.) deep.

About 200 yards (180 m.) west of Tayavalla, the Roman line is crossed by a modern road (Maryfield Place), west of which the Ditch may be seen running on westwards through the Tentfield Plantation. It is preserved in good condition, sometimes in very good condition, for about $1\frac{1}{2}$ miles (2·4 km.), in the course of which its line is interrupted only by the track of a disused mineral railway and by a great clay bing or mound. About 150 yards (140 m.) west of the beginning of the Tentfield Plantation may be seen the remains of one of the turf platforms attached to the rear of the Wall, and there are barely discernible traces of another about 50 yards (45 m.) east of the mineral railway. Farther west, beyond the great clay mound, a fine section of the Antonine Wall, Ditch and outer mound was exposed to view by the Scottish Gas Board in 1959. The Wall was 15 feet (4·5 m.) wide at the base and the Ditch about 40 feet (c. 12 m.) wide. There is a stone marker at the place where this section was opened up (Fig. 4B).

ROUGH CASTLE TO SEABEGS (Fig. 11)

The fort at Rough Castle was the second smallest fort, as far as is known, on the Antonine Wall, its internal area being only about 1 acre (·4 h.). It is now the best preserved of all the Antonine Wall forts. The Scottish Development Department has been engaged in clearing operations and excavation work on the site with the aim of rendering the outlines of the fort more distinct, and of throwing more light on its history.

Even now the remains are impressive indeed. The Antonine Wall and Ditch are very well preserved along the north front of the fort, and the fort rampart and ditches and

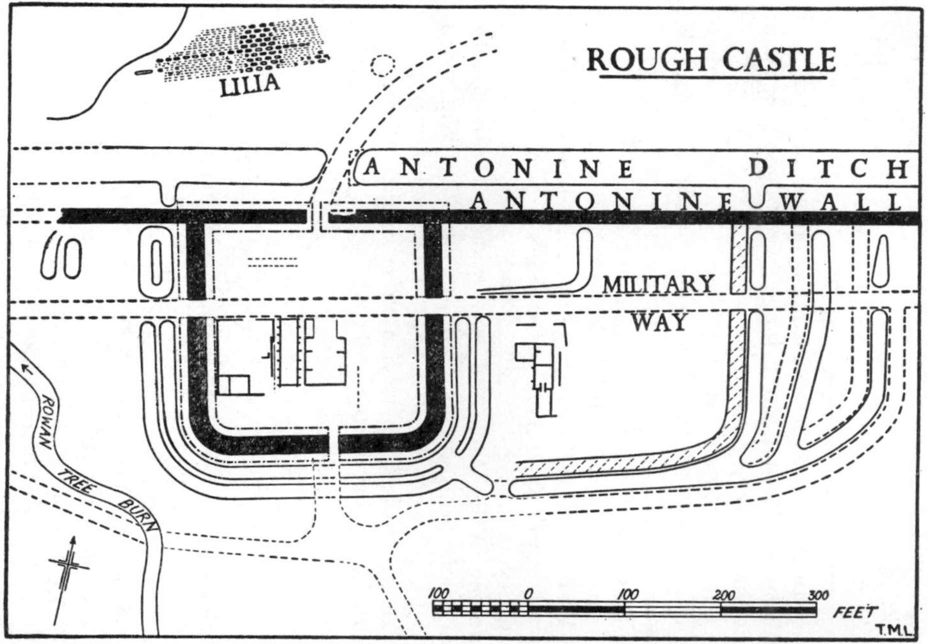

ROUGH CASTLE

ANTONINE DITCH

ANTONINE WALL

LILIA

MILITARY WAY

ROWAN TREE BURN

100   0   100   200   300

FEET

TML

FIGURE II

the annexe ditches are very clearly visible on the east, south and west sides.

Excavations carried out at Rough Castle in 1902-1903, and resumed 30 years later by Sir George Macdonald, have shown that the Antonine Wall base was here c. 15 feet (4·5 m.) wide and appeared to have been laid down before the fort was completed. The Antonine Ditch, 40 feet (12 m.) wide, did however have a gap for a causeway opposite the north gateway. The fort rampart was about 20 feet (6 m.) wide at the base, and there were two ditches on the west and south sides and one (later two) on the south half of the east front. Outside the north half of the east front there was a small enclosure, which stood inside a very large annexe attached to the fort on its east side and defended by a rampart and ditch.

In the centre of the fort there were identified the remains of a Headquarters Building, much smaller than usual, one granary and another stone building which may have been the Officers' Quarters. Outside the fort in the annexe stood the bath-house.

In a hole (possibly the well) in the Headquarters Building there were found three fragments of an inscribed tablet recording the erection of the Headquarters Building by the Sixth Cohort of Nervii. Men of the same cohort also set up an altar to the goddess Victory, which was found a little to the south of the fort in 1843. These men were under the command, not of an auxiliary commander, but of a centurion of the Twentieth Legion, Flavius Betto by name.

The fort at Rough Castle had undergone alterations and modifications in plan at least once during the Antonine occupation. Still clearly visible on the ground today are three ditches on the east side of the annexe, which seem to be separated from one another by the remains of turf ramparts. These appear unlikely to have all belonged to the original defence plan.

There seem to have been alterations in the course taken by the Military Way. At first it appears to have pursued a straight course right through the annexe and the fort down the slope to the Rowan Tree Burn and up the opposite bank. Later, it seems, it was supplied with a loop or by-pass skirting the southern defences of annexe and fort. At the south gate of the fort, too, yet another by-pass seems to have approached from the south. It is possible to follow the line of the Military Way almost all the way from the north-east corner of the annexe to the south-east corner of the fort.

To the north-west of the Antonine fort there is a remarkable series of ten rows of defensive pits—*lilia* or lilies—about 20 or 30 yards (18-27 m.) beyond the Antonine Ditch. With stakes planted in them, and with twigs and leaves strewn over them, they would present the appearance of solid ground, only to throw into confusion any who set foot on them.

If approached by road, the fort site at Rough Castle is most easily reached, not from the east, but from the west. A road over the Forth-Clyde Canal at Bonnybridge leads, with a few sharp turns, to Bonnyside House. A lane runs onwards to a gate on the left (or north) giving access to a footpath and a road for cars. A footpath to the south of the visitors' car park runs eastwards to the fort site, high on its steep slope above the Rowan Tree Burn. For some distance the path is on the line of the Military Way.

When leaving the fort and following the line of the Antonine barrier westwards, the visitor will not only see the Ditch stretching ahead of him in fine condition for about half a mile (·8 km.), but he will detect also, to the south of it, the well-preserved remains of the Antonine Wall in the form of a turf-covered mound standing to a height of about 5 feet (1·5 m.). Several sections have been cut on the line of the Wall in this area from 1890 onwards. In 1970 and 1971, two old sections were reopened, cleaned, drawn and photographed.

At a distance of about ¼-mile (·4 km.) west of Rough Castle there are the remains of one of the signalling platforms attached to the back of the Wall. It is just inside the stone wall bordering the north edge of the lane running west to Bonnyside House. The lane here lies over the Military Way. During excavation at this point in 1957 Dr. K. Steer discovered a gravel pit, dug during the construction of the Military Way, under the 17-foot (5 m.) square signalling platform. Another platform may be seen just inside the grounds of Bonnyside House, and between the two platforms there are surface traces of more gravel pits.

At Bonnyside House, a glance westwards shows the reed-filled hollow of the Ditch running straight on with a low mound to south (now surmounted by a pylon) marking the site of the Wall itself, and another low mound to the north representing the upcast from the Ditch. Beyond, loom the Kilsyth Hills. In 1932 and 1977, at Seabegs Motte, the north kerb of the Antonine Wall base and the south lip of the Ditch were located.

The line of Wall and Ditch may be picked up next on the west side of Bonnybridge, where they are now closely followed by a secondary road from Bonnybridge to Castle-cary (B816) which runs parallel to the Forth-Clyde Canal on its south side. The hollow of the Ditch may be seen at the foot of the garden of the farm called Seabegs Place, just on the south side of the road.

SEABEGS TO CASTLECARY (Fig. 12)

Towards the end of the seventeenth century, there were noticed the remains of " a great Fort at the east end of Seabegwood ". The small plateau with its wide outlook above the little stream at the east end of Seabegs Wood would be a suitable site and would have been large enough to accommodate a small fort. Trenching in 1968-1972 failed to locate it, although the Antonine Wall base was found.

The line of Wall, Ditch and outer mound are well preserved for a stretch of $\frac{1}{4}$-mile (·4 km.) within Seabegs Wood, the Ditch having a width of over 40 feet (12 m.) and a depth of 6-8 feet (c. 2 m.). Even the Military Way may be detected. A trench cut across it in 1962 proved it to be 23 feet (7 m.) wide.

In 1977, in the field at the west end of Seabegs Wood, Mr. L. J. F. Keppie and Mr. J. Walker discovered a fortlet attached to the rear of the Antonine Wall, and of one build with it. It measured internally c. 73 by 60 feet (21·8 m. by 18 m.), and was defended by a turf rampart on a stone base 10 feet (3 m.) wide, and by two ditches. There was no gap in the Antonine Ditch at the north gate of the fortlet.

SEABEGS WOOD FORTLET

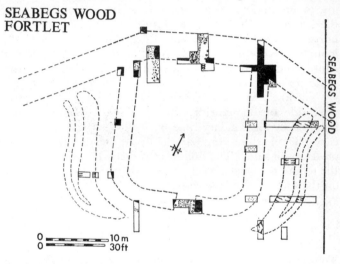

0 —————— 10 m
0 —————— 30 ft

SEABEGS WOOD

FIGURE 12

There seemed to have been two periods of occupation (Fig. 12).

Beyond the west end of the wood, the hollow of the Ditch may be seen descending to the modern road, only to be obliterated by the Canal which has usurped its line for about 300 yards (270 m.) westwards. At a point opposite Underwood House, Canal, Ditch and modern road diverge again, the Ditch becoming faintly visible from time to time in the fields and gardens on the north side of the road.

Just to the west of a bowling green, on the north side of

the road, the Ditch once more becomes prominent and may
be followed, either by eye from the road, or on foot, as far
as a dip in the wall of the grounds of former Castlecary
School. Here the road swings sharply north-west to join the
main Stirling-Glasgow road (A80), leaving to the south the
stone-walled fort of Castlecary. This is reached by following a road marked " Walton " which runs south from the
Bonnybridge to Castlecary road (B816), and then by
turning east.

CASTLECARY TO WESTERWOOD (Figs. 13, 14)

Castlecary fort has suffered greatly during the last two
centuries, having been robbed for building stone during the
construction of the Forth-Clyde Canal about 1770 and
having been ruthlessly cut across by the Edinburgh-
Glasgow railway about 1840. It was excavated in 1902,
and, as at Rough Castle, the intense public interest in the
excavations led to their being left open, with results ruinous
to the stonework and other remains. The north, east and
west sides can, however, still be distinguished.

The fort was defended by a stone wall, 8 feet (2·4 m.)
wide, whose squared north corners made provision for a
junction with the Antonine Wall, here 14·5 feet (4·4 m.) wide
at the base. The Antonine Ditch shrank from a width of
40 feet (12 m.) to a width of 15 feet (4·5 m.) west of the
north gateway of the fort. The fort had an internal area of
about 3·5 acres (1·4 h.), and had two ditches on east, south
and west sides. There was an annexe on the east side, about
2·75 acres (1·1 h.) in internal area, defended by a rampart
and a ditch.

Stone buildings identified within the fort included the
Headquarters Building and a granary in the central block,
a bath-house in the south-east sector and a latrine just
inside the north-east corner. A road has also been traced,
entering the south gate of the fort, and coming up from the
south, possibly a branch from the Clyde valley road.

Two legionary detachments and two auxiliary cohorts

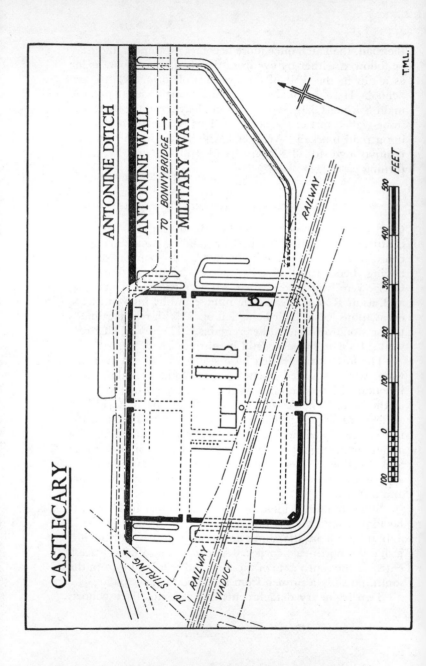

CASTLECARY

ANTONINE DITCH

ANTONINE WALL

TO BONNYBRIDGE →

MILITARY WAY

TO STIRLING

RAILWAY

VIADUCT

RAILWAY

RAILWAY

FEET

100   0   100   200   300   400   500

TML.

have left records of their presence at Castlecary. An altar found about 1769 in the bath-house had been dedicated to Fortuna by detachments of the Second and Sixth Legions, and another altar found just west of the fort was set up to Mercury by men of the Sixth Legion. A building inscription found in 1764 recorded construction work by the First Cohort of Tungri, 1,000 strong, and another altar found west of the fort, near the altar to Mercury, was dedicated to Neptune by the First Cohort of Vardulli, 1,000 strong with a mounted contingent. These two cohorts could hardly have occupied the fort if they were at full strength, since it had an internal area of only 3·5 acres (1·4 h.).

Besides these stones the harvest of finds from Castlecary included Antonine pottery and coins, and glass and several potsherds of first-century date. Here there may have been an Agricolan fort, although structural remains of it have not yet been identified.

For some distance west of Castlecary fort the line of Wall and Ditch has been destroyed by the main road from Glasgow to Stirling (A80), and by the railway viaduct. A well-preserved stretch of the Ditch north of Castlecary Village may be approached from the east or west, either by taking a side-road (signposted " Garnhall ") running north from the secondary Glasgow to Castlecary road, or by entering the northern end of another side-road where it runs off the secondary Glasgow-Kilsyth-Stirling road (A803). At a point on this latter side-road where it makes two right-angled bends, the Ditch is crossed, and may be seen quite clearly from the road, running eastwards and westwards. The eastward stretch will be seen to even better advantage by leaving the Castlecary road (B816) at the west end of Castlecary Village and following the approach road to Garnhall Farm.

Excavation on this stretch in 1977 showed the Antonine Ditch and Wall base to be very well preserved, with evidence for the junction of two working squads and of repair to the base. There is a proposal to use Garnhall Farm buildings as a visitor centre for the Wall line.

The stretch of the Ditch westwards from Garnhall is so well-preserved, lying partly in a grove of trees, that it should be followed on foot if possible. In 1964, a stretch of the Wall base was traced from Tollpark westwards. Just opposite a little hollow in the north slope of the Ditch, the stone base is still visible.

The Ditch is here 6-7 feet (c. 2 m.) deep and well over 40 feet (12 m.) wide and it continues in fine preservation for well over a mile (1·6 km.), being crossed by grassy tracks or " old roads " which admit of approach to the line on foot. For a distance of over ¼-mile (·4 km.) in fact, one of these farm tracks lies on the line of the Military Way. The two diverge again, however, west of the lonely ruined hamlet of Arniebog. About ¼-mile (·4 km.) west of Arniebog, the Ditch may be seen passing in front of the (former) farmhouse of Westerwood.

WESTERWOOD TO CROY HILL (Figs. 14, 15)

Westerwood farmhouse and steading lie within the north-east angle of the Antonine fort. It stood on a slight slope, with a fairly steep descent to north, and its outlines can still be faintly discerned. Excavation by Sir George Macdonald in 1932 showed that the Antonine Wall base was here 14 feet (4·3 m.) wide, and that it had been overlapped, slightly, by the east and west rampart bases of the fort. Clearly the Wall base had been laid down first, but a gap had been left or made in it for the north fort gateway. On the other hand, the Ditch, here about 40 feet (12 m.) wide, had swept past the fort without a break, as if it had been dug first of all.

For most of its length the fort rampart had been 16 feet (4·8 m.) wide, and had enclosed an area of almost 1·95 acres (·78 h.). There had been two ditches on the east, west and south sides, the two south ditches passing the south gate without a break. On the northern half of the west side the ditches were increased to three in number. Part of only one stone building has been uncovered. It stood inside the north-west angle and was probably a bath-house.

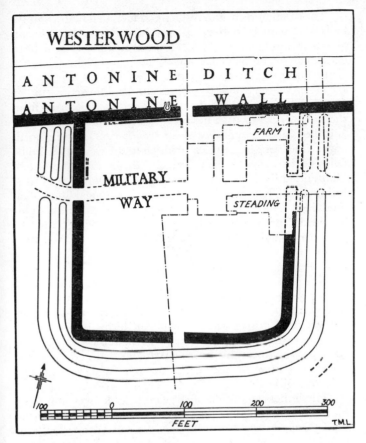

WESTERWOOD

ANTONINE DITCH

ANTONINE WALL

FARM

MILITARY

WAY STEADING

N

100   0   100   200   300
FEET   T.M.L.

FIGURE 14

The Military Way has been traced from Arniebog straight on through the fort at Westerwood and for over ¼-mile (·4 km.) westwards. Just outside the south-east corner of the fort another short stretch of road was found. It may be part of a loop or by-pass. Excavation in 1974 to the south of the fort-site revealed no traces of an extra-mural settlement.

63

The small finds from Westerwood included many ballista balls and a little pottery of Antonine date. In 1963 an altar was ploughed up west of the fort-site. It had been dedicated to the Silvanae and Quadruae by the wife of a centurion in the Sixth Legion.

From Westerwood, the Ditch can be followed easily for over ¼-mile (·4 km.), as it descends gently westwards from the fort. A grassy path lies for a short distance in the Ditch and then inclines slightly northwards to run along its north edge. The very fine stretch of Ditch to the west may also be followed by crossing to a grassy path south of the Ditch. Obliterated for a short distance by the embankment of the Edinburgh-Glasgow railway, the Ditch reappears first of all on the left hand side of a minor road, and then on its right-hand side, in both places heavily overgrown with trees. In this area, remains of the Wall and of the Military Way were uncovered in 1958. In 1975-6 two temporary camps were excavated to the south of Dullatur House.

North of Dullatur Railway Station, the well-marked hollow of the Ditch comes into view again. A little farther westwards it is crossed by the Cumbernauld-Dullatur-Kilsyth road, to the west of which it forms the boundary between two fields, with a stone wall set in the bottom of it. After passing through a narrow strip of woodland the Ditch becomes visible in the fields beyond as a well-defined hollow.

The imposing stretch of the Ditch to the west, on Croy Hill, is best approached by turning off the Dullatur-Kilsyth road through a gate a little way west of Wester Dullatur farmhouse. The gate opens on to a track which leads up to the old embankment of a disused mineral railway. From the embankment there is a fine view along the Ditch both eastwards to Dullatur and westwards up the eastern shoulder of Croy Hill. " For nearly a mile onwards," remarked Sir George Macdonald, " a descriptive account is scarcely required. Those who are able to visit the sector for themselves will need no guide, so conspicuous are the remains."

64

Although the Antonine Wall itself and the Military Way are hardly discernible, the Ditch is wonderfully preserved. It is seen to best advantage by walking along its north edge or counterscarp until the point is reached where an 80-foot (25 m.) long stretch of the Ditch was never dug. As Alexander Gordon said, this " serves as it were, for a Bridge to pass from one Side to the other ". There is also a well-marked grassy path on the south side of the Ditch. Between the railway embankment and the break in the Ditch, its dimensions now average about 40 feet (12 m.) in width and 8 feet (2·4 m.) in depth.

CROY HILL TO BAR HILL (Figs. 15, 16)

Immediately to the west of the break in the Antonine Ditch, there had stood a small fort on a plateau about 400 feet (120 m.) above sea-level with a rapid slope to north, east and south, and an extensive view eastwards to the Firth of Forth and the hills of Fife, northwards to the Kilsyth Hills, and westwards to the next fort on Bar Hill. This is one of the highest points on the line.

Roman stones were long ago recorded from Croy Hill, including many building stones tooled with diamond and other patterns, which were noted by the Glasgow Archaeological Society's Antonine Wall Committee when cutting sections across the Wall and Ditch on Croy Hill. Excavations conducted by Sir George Macdonald in 1920, 1931, and 1935 recovered much of the plan of the fort.

As at Westerwood, the base of the Antonine Wall, here 14 feet (4·3 m.) wide, had been laid down first, with a break left or made in it for the north gate of the fort, and the fort rampart base overlapped the Wall base slightly, at least on the west side. A short stretch of cobbled road lay outside the north gate, but there was no break in the Ditch, here 40 feet (12 m.) wide. There was of course the 80-foot (25 m.) long " Bridge " to the east of the fort. The internal area was 1·5 acres (·6 h.), and there were two or three ditches along the west and south sides of the fort, but only

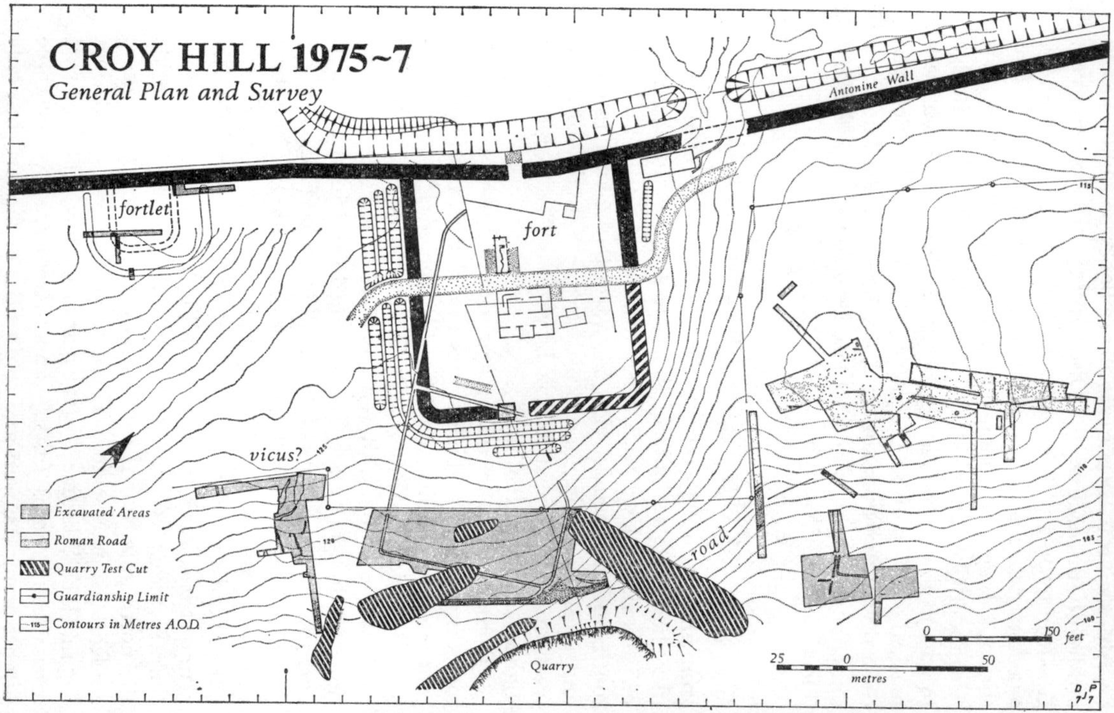
CROY HILL 1975~7
General Plan and Survey
Antonine Wall
fortlet
fort
vicus?
road
Quarry
Excavated Areas
Roman Road
Quarry Test Cut
Guardianship Limit
Contours in Metres A.O.D.
0
150 feet
25
0
50
metres

FIGURE 15

one on the north part of the east front, and none on the south part of that front or on the east part of the south front.

In the centre of the fort were found the remains of the Headquarters Building and a granary. In the north-east corner there was a remarkable stone-built well, later built over by a corner tower. Just outside the north-east corner stood a bath-house. There was noted, as at Mumrills and Rough Castle, evidence for alterations and modifications in certain of the fort-buildings.

The finds made from time to time on Croy Hill establish the presence there of a detachment of the Sixth Legion. These included a building stone of that legion (and two other fragments), and an altar set up to the Nymphs. Croy Hill, like Westerwood, has produced many ballista balls.

Under the Antonine Wall fort on Croy Hill, Sir George Macdonald found a ditch surrounding a small enclosure of about $\frac{3}{4}$ acre (·3 h.), with an annexe of about the same area to the south of it. This, thought by him to be of Agricolan date, now seems likely to have been a proto-Antonine enclosure housing a construction unit.

Excavation by Mr. W. S. Hanson in 1975-1978 has suggested that the work of the construction unit was the building of a fortlet on a plateau about 250 feet (80 m.) to the west of Croy Hill fort. The fortlet measured internally c. 62 feet (18·5 m.) from east to west, and c. 73·5 feet (22 m.) from north to south. It was defended by a ditch and by a turf rampart on a stone base, of contemporary build with the Antonine Wall and its stone base. The fortlet was later replaced by Croy Hill fort.

Mr. Hanson's excavations also revealed that a civil settlement lay south-west of the fort, and that the area east of the fort had been used for agricultural or industrial activity. He also confirmed the line of a bypass road south of the fort.

West of the fort, the Antonine Ditch swings to the north " to wind along the face of the hill through what Gordon calls ' a long continued Track of Rocks and frightful Precipices ' ". Though the descent to the north is steep and at times precipitous, the Ditch has been hewn with inflexible determination out of no less inflexible rock—a monument to " Roman Resolution and Grandeur ".

For a considerable distance west of the fort, a grassy track runs on top of the Wall, as it rises to the true summit of Croy Hill, 470 feet (c. 145 m.) above sea-level, and descends again rather rapidly towards Croy village. In this stretch, the Military Way has been traced westwards from the fort and was found to have been joined by another road coming through a gap in the low hills to the south. This second road is probably the end of a long loop line which left the main Military Way much farther east.

A little farther west there are two turf-built stone-based platforms attached to the rear of the Wall. Cuttings were made through both of them by the late nineteenth-century Antonine Wall Committee. In one cutting the turf super-structure of the Wall was still standing to a height of over 5 feet (1·5m.) and the "batter" or slope of the turf was clearly visible. In 1967 this cutting was reopened, drawn and photographed.

On the east border of the village of Croy the line of the Antonine Wall and Ditch has been wiped out by quarrying, but trenching in 1931 revealed the stone base surviving in good preservation for some distance on either side of it. The Wall ran straight on, being crossed first by the Nethercroy Road and secondly by the Kilsyth-Croy road (B802). A modern track running westwards from this road to Bar Hill has kept very close to the line of Wall and Ditch, being laid partly in the Ditch and partly over its south edge. In the wood—Girnal Hill Wood—to the south of the track, the Military Way was exposed to view at several points in 1931. Further on, the right fork of the track directs the eye and the feet onwards towards Castle Hill, with its Trig. Point.

Just before the modern track leads into Forestry Commission property, it bends to the south, leaving the line of the Wall and Ditch. One of the fine sections cut farther west by the Glasgow Archaeological Society's Antonine Wall Committee showed the Ditch to have been 12 feet

(3·6 m.) deep and almost 40 feet (12 m.) wide, and the Wall base to have been 15·5 feet (4·7 m.) wide.

Within the Forestry Commission plantation, the Ditch may be followed by keeping close to the northern limit of the planted area. For the next ¼-mile (·4 km.) or more the Ditch has a stone wall set in it, and south of it the line of the Wall base was precisely determined in 1957. Its width was usually 14 feet (4·3 m.). As they sweep round the shoulder of Castle Hill the Wall and Ditch reach one of the highest points on the line—a height of 475 feet (145 m.) above sea-level. From the top of Castle Hill itself, 30 feet (9 m.) higher, a fortunate visitor may, on a very clear day, catch a glimpse of the water of both Firths—Forth and Clyde.

Lying about 200 yards (180 m.) westwards from Castle Hill is another hill, Bar Hill, now supporting a fine grove of trees which does not, however, obscure the outlines of an Antonine Wall fort or the line of the Wall. The Ditch, too, may be followed by a resolute pedestrian.

BAR HILL TO AUCHENDAVY (Fig. 16)

The fort on Bar Hill is most conveniently reached from the west by crossing the Canal at Twechar, on the secondary Kilsyth-Kirkintilloch road (B8023), and turning off east-wards at the War Memorial along a farm road which leads towards the grove on Bar Hill. A track running along the south edge of the grove is on the line of the southern defences of the fort, and a diversion northwards should bring the visitor to the well near the centre of the fort.

Extensive excavations were carried out at Bar Hill in 1902-1905 by Sir George Macdonald and Mr. Alexander Park, at the expense of the then owner of the land, Mr. Alexander Whitelaw of Gartshore. It was the highest fort on the line, lying 495 feet (c. 150 m.) above sea-level, and in Roman times it had a magnificent outlook not only to north but also eastwards and westwards far along the line of the Antonine frontier.

The Bar Hill fort had not used the Antonine Wall as its

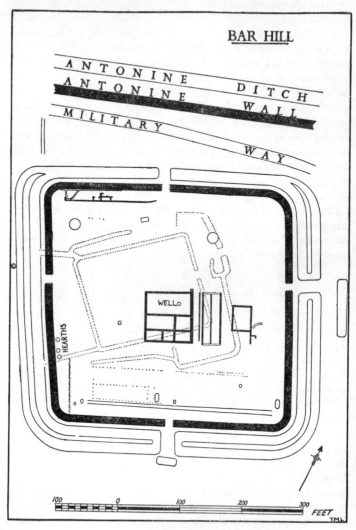

BAR HILL

ANTONINE DITCH

ANTONINE WALL

MILITARY WAY

WELLo

HEARTHS

100   0   100   200   300 FEET

FIGURE 16

northern defence, since it lay detached from the Wall, about 100 feet (30 m.) to the south of it. A branch of the Military Way had in fact swung north before reaching the east gate of the fort, to pass between the fort and the Wall. It was there about 17 feet wide (5 m.), with a camber, and with gutters at each side.

The fort had an internal area of 3·2 acres (1·3 h.) and was defended by a turf rampart 12 feet (3·6 m.) wide at the base, by two ditches on the east, south and west sides, and by one ditch on the north side. The two west ditches were not interrupted at the west gate, and the south and east gates were masked by short detached lengths of ditch. As the fort stood apart from the Wall, all its corners were rounded. The two west ditches, the rounded north-west corner and a culvert piercing the north rampart, west of the north-east corner, may all be distinguished today.

Inside the fort were found the remains of the Head-quarters Building, a granary and another stone building, all in the central block, besides a bath-house inside the north-west angle (exposed to view in 1978), and also a water tank, streets, postholes of wooden barrack blocks (many with the stumps of posts still in them), and several pits. The most impressive of all the structural remains were those of the well, in the courtyard of the Headquarters Building. It was 43 feet (13 m.) deep and 4 feet (1·2 m.) in diameter, and it was steined or " cradled " all the way down with shaped stones. Original Roman stones from the well have been used to rebuild the present well-mouth.

It was from the well that there came the most remark-able of the objects in the rich harvest of finds from Bar Hill (which have all been recently re-examined and published in detail). For its whole depth the well had been choked with debris, apparently thrown in when the fort was abandoned. There were an altar and three fragments of a building inscription set up by the First Cohort of Baetasii; over twenty columns, bases and capitals; building stones; ballista balls; wooden beams; part of the pulley of the well and the well-bucket; leather articles; great masses of iron weapons and tools; bronze ornaments; animal bones and shells; and (at the bottom) 13 coins. Ten of these coins were of tin, cast in moulds instead of being struck, and they were probably made on the spot to be thrown into the well as offerings.

The First Cohort of Baetasii was not the only auxiliary unit to be associated with Bar Hill. The presence of the First Cohort of Hamii (Syrian archers), 500 strong, had previously been attested by an altar to Silvanus and a tomb-stone, and was confirmed by the discovery of some fragments of bows during the 1902-1905 excavations. Detachments of the Second and Twentieth Legions have also recorded building activity at Bar Hill.

The altar to Silvanus was ploughed up, in 1895, 240 yards (c. 215 m.) north-east of the east gate of the fort. It may have stood in a shrine erected outside the fort in an annexe. Although the defences or limits of such an annexe have not been defined, yet the discovery, to the south and east of the fort, of an outlying stretch of ditch, as well as fireplaces and many potsherds, indicate the existence of extra-mural settlement.

In 1976 a long-lost altar to Silvanus, formerly attributed to Cadder, was found in the ruins of a 17th-century house at Kilsyth, less than 2 miles (3 km.) north of Bar Hill. It probably came from Bar Hill. During the 1902-1905 excavations, silted and over-grown ditches of an earlier fort were found under the Antonine Headquarters Building, and when traced were found to have enclosed an area of about half an acre (·2 h.). The ditch system was elaborate, apparently designed to shelter the single, east, entrance to the fort, and there was a small annexe to west. The fact that the small fort faced east and lay askew to the Antonine Wall, suggests a pre-Antonine date for it.

From Bar Hill the line of the Ditch may be followed, with some difficulty owing to the clinging nature of the thick undergrowth with which it is filled, towards the Canal Bridge at Twechar. Between the farmhouse of Shirva, about 600 yards (540 m.) west of the Canal Bridge, and the farm of Auchendavy, the modern road (B8023) keeps in close company with the Antonine Wall and Ditch.

In or beside a so-called " tumulus " near Shirva, there were found in the early eighteenth century at least three Roman tombstones and two uninscribed slabs each showing a dead man reclining at a sepulchral banquet, as well as a building stone set up by a detachment of the Second Legion. The tombstones probably came from the cemetery of a fort at either Bar Hill or Auchendavy. The three which have survived were set up over Flavius Lucianus, a private soldier in the Second Legion, a fifteen-year-old boy, Salmanes, and a lady, Verecunda.

AUCHENDAVY TO KIRKINTILLOCH

The existence of a fort at Auchendavy has long been known, and its east ditches and south-east angle have recently been detected from the air by Professor St. Joseph. The area of the fort is now bisected by the Kilsyth-Auchinstarry-Kirkintilloch road (B8023) which here may override the Military Way, and within it there lies the farmhouse of Auchendavy, north of the road, with the farm steading south of the road. It is probable that the Forth-Clyde Canal has partly destroyed the southern defences of the fort.

It was during the construction of the Canal, in 1771, that there came to light the most remarkable of the many chance finds (including many ballista balls) which have been recorded from Auchendavy. In a pit, apparently lying just south of the fort, there were found four altars, part of a fifth, a stone bust, and two iron mallets. The altars and bust survive, and four of the altars prove to have been set up by the same man, Marcus Cocceius Firmus, a centurion of the Second Legion, to no fewer than eleven different deities, or groups of deities. The fifth altar, broken, no longer bears the name of the dedicator, but only the name of the deity, Silvanus.

Between Auchendavy and the centre of Kirkintilloch, the Wall and Ditch are hardly visible. In 1963, however, the Ditch was located about 1 mile (1·6 km.) east of Kirkintilloch. The stone base of the Wall was, too, exposed in the stackyard of Cleddans Farm in 1909, and in 1975 in Hillhead Road. In 1958 the line of the Ditch was established at Cleddans and about 300 yards (270 m.) to the west.

West of this point, the line has been obscured by the growth of Kirkintilloch, and trenching in 1952 failed to discover any traces of the Wall base or Ditch. In all probability the Roman line lay further north than anticipated, on the brow of the hill, passing under, or just north of, the Old Kirk of Kirkintilloch, which has recently been transformed into The Auld Kirk Museum.

Kirkintilloch to Cadder

In the Peel Park, Kirkintilloch, just west of the Old Kirk, there stands a fairly well preserved example of a mediaeval peel with a surrounding moat, possibly dating back to the twelfth century A.D. This the early antiquaries accepted, with almost complete unanimity, as a Roman fort, and they supposed that it projected, surprisingly, into enemy country to the north of the Antonine Wall.

Discoveries of Roman building stones, a quern stone, a clay jar and Roman coins have long ago been recorded from the neighbourhood of the Peel; they pointed to the existence of a fort nearby. In 1914, Sir George Macdonald cut trenches in the Park west of the Peel and discovered some hearths, along with tiles and Roman pottery. In the years between 1953 and 1961 trenching revealed the stone base of the Antonine Wall, about 15 feet (4·5 m.) wide, and the Antonine Ditch, at least 35 feet (10·5 m.) wide, at the north-west corner of the Peel Park, and in two gardens immediately west of it. Inside the Park there were found to the south of the Antonine Wall remains of streets, gutters and several rows of postholes, belonging to narrow wooden

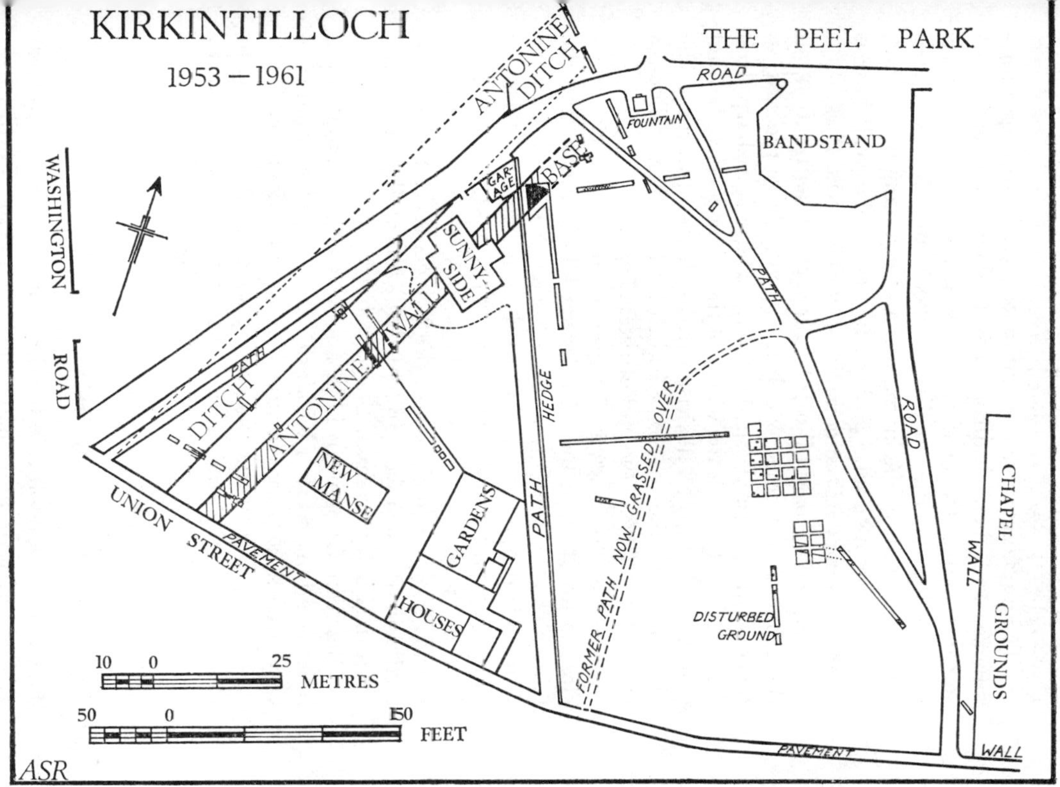

KIRKINTILLOCH
1953—1961

THE PEEL PARK

CHAPEL GROUNDS

WALL

WALL

ROAD

BANDSTAND

ROAD

PATH

FOUNTAIN

DISTURBED GROUNDS

FORMER PATH NOW GRASSED OVER

ANTONINE DITCH

BASE

BASE

HEDGE

PATH

SUNNY-SIDE

GARDENS

HOUSES

ANTONINE WALL

NEW MANSE

DITCH

UNION STREET

PAVEMENT

WASHINGTON

ROAD

PAVEMENT

METRES

FEET

25

50

10   0

50   0

ASR

FIGURE 17

buildings, besides a great quantity of Antonine pottery (Fig. 17).

These remains indicate the presence of a fort, or a fort-annexe, and their disturbed condition at the same time suggests that much of the fort has been destroyed by the construction of the mediaeval peel and its associated structures, and by the laying out and terracing of the Park in more recent times. A short stretch of the Wall base is exposed to view in the north-west corner of the Park.

The fort at Kirkintilloch had a very strong position, on the top of a long ridge which rises gently from the east, to descend more steeply on the west. There is a sharp drop on the north towards the valley of the River Kelvin, beyond which the Campsie Hills rise threateningly upwards. The old form of the name Kirkintilloch—Cairpentalloch—means " the fort at the end of the ridge ".

The modern Kilsyth-Glasgow road (A803) runs very close to the Roman line as it leaves Kirkintilloch, and the faint hollow of the Ditch may be seen in the fields on the south side of the road as far as the Canal Bridge (Glasgow Bridge) and then on the north side of the road. The Roman Wall changed direction sharply at this point and here, to the south of the road, east of the Bridge, there had stood a fortlet, c. 60 by 70 feet (18 by 21 m.) internally, discovered from the air by Professor St. Joseph.

Between Glasgow Bridge and a traffic roundabout 2 miles (3·2 km.) west of Kirkintilloch the modern road runs very straight and may actually lie over the Military Way. At the roundabout the road swings south-west on its way to Glasgow but the line of the Military Way is continued, approximately, by a narrow belt of trees.

CADDER TO BALMUILDY (Fig. 18)

The belt of trees points in the direction of the site of the fort at Cadder, long ago encroached on by the Forth-Clyde Canal, and now completely destroyed by a sand quarry. It

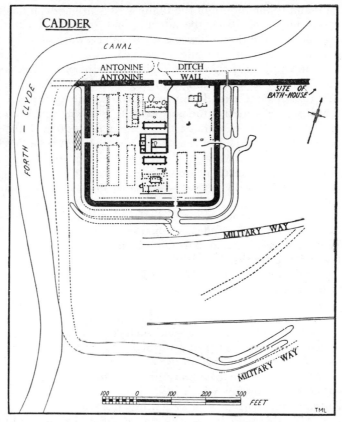

FIGURE 18

was extensively excavated by Mr. J. Clarke in the years
1929-1931.

The site of Cadder fort is naturally strong with " slopes
to the north, south and west. To the north in particular the
ground falls away very steeply to the meadows bordering
the River Kelvin, which even today are at times flooded,
and before modern drainage must have been a morass. In
this direction there is a clear view across to the Campsie

Hills and to the mouth of the Blane Valley from which any hostile movement from the north would emerge. To the east alone is the position weak ". It was no doubt for this reason that the fort at Cadder faced east.

The width of the Antonine Ditch in front of the fort is unknown, since it was long ago dug into during the construction of the Canal, but it was certainly interrupted for the passage of a road at the north gate. The Antonine Wall seemed to have been about 15·5 feet (4·7 m.) wide at the base, as was also the fort rampart. There were two ditches on the east and south sides of the fort and one on the west side. This west ditch at first had no break in it, but was later provided with a causeway. The internal area was 2·8 acres (1·12 h.).

The central block of buildings faced east, and included stone Headquarters, Officers' Quarters, and two granaries. Wooden barracks stood in front and behind, and there were two suites of baths, one inside the north-east angle of the fort and one outside the fort to the east. Evidence was forthcoming for alterations in plan on at least one occasion during the Antonine period.

As the fort faced east, the Military Way did not pass through it, but skirted the south defences closely. It also sent off two loops as it approached from the east. Both loops may not have been in use together.

Mr. Clarke's excavations at Cadder also produced structural evidence which suggested to him that the Antonine fort had been preceded by an Agricolan occupation. To this may have belonged a palisade trench and outlying ditches which had no connection with the Antonine fort. Although these might have been proto-Antonine rather than Agricolan, there is a little pottery of the late first century A.D. from Cadder. The Antonine finds include a building stone of the Second Legion.

West of Cadder the Roman line is most easily re-joined by following a side road—Balmuildy Road—northwards from the Kilsyth-Glasgow road (A803). Balmuildy Road soon makes a right-angled turn westwards to run along the north side of Wilderness Plantation, with the Antonine Wall and Ditch to the north. Their exact line was established by trenching in 1963. In this stretch there were three sub-rectangular ditched enclosures and a fortlet set near a point where the Wall and Ditch changed direction. Excavation in 1965 and 1966 showed that the fortlet had been defended by a turf rampart on a stone base 10 feet (3 m.) wide and by two ditches on the east, west and south sides. Internally it measured c. 65 feet (19·5 m.) by 60 feet (18 m.). Its north rampart was of one build with the Antonine Wall, but there was no break in the Ditch.

For about a mile between Wilderness Plantation and Easter Balmuildy, the road accompanies the Roman line, the hollow of the Ditch becoming well defined just north of Easter Balmuildy farmhouse, immediately east of the site of Balmuildy fort. Trenching in 1973-4 to the east of Easter Balmuildy determined the line of Wall and Ditch.

BALMUILDY TO BEARSDEN (Fig. 19)

The site of Balmuildy fort is cut through by the road from Glasgow to Balmore via Lambhill (A879). The greater part of the fort lies on the east side of the road, on the south bank of the Kelvin, but its south-west sector is on the west side of the road, in the farmland of Wester Balmuildy.

The remains of the fort long survived in good condition to engage the interest of antiquaries, but its outlines are hardly to be discerned today. Of the many Roman stones accidentally discovered on the site down to the nineteenth century, only one—or rather part of one—has survived. This is Alexander Gordon's " most invaluable Jewel of Antiquity ", recording building work done by the Second Legion in the governorship of Lollius Urbicus.

The building work recorded was doubtless the construction of Balmuildy fort. Mr. S. N. Miller's excavations there, during the years 1912-1914, showed that the fort

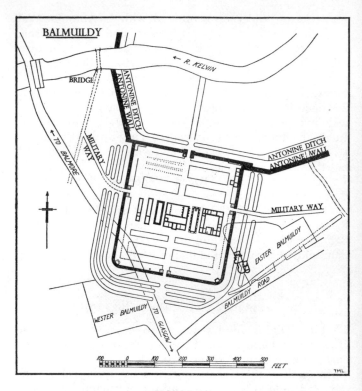

FIGURE 19

(4 acres (1·6 h.) in internal area) had been enclosed on all four sides by a stone wall, about 7 feet (2·1 m.) wide. Some courses of the wall, as well as its foundations, still survived. The south corners of the fort were rounded, but the north corners were squared in anticipation of the junction with them of the Antonine Wall. From the two north corners, projecting stone wings were thrown out to meet the Wall. When it did arrive, the turf Wall, 14-15 feet (c. 4·5 m.) wide with sloping sides, was not joined on to the 7-foot (2·1 m.) wide, straight-sided stone wings. Instead, the Wall was tucked in behind the stone wing at the north-east corner,

80

and started off at a sharp angle from the northern face of the stone wing at the north-west corner.

On the north front of the fort the Antonine Ditch was only about 12-13 feet (3·7 m.) wide, although it was over 20 feet (6 m.) wide on either side of the fort. This has suggested that the fort-builders also dug the stretch of the Ditch north of the fort, as well as erecting the stone wall round the fort, before the Wall-builders arrived. There were two ditches on the east side of the fort, and three on the south and west sides. The four gates were each guarded by two watch-towers, the remains of the watch-towers at the north gate being particularly well-preserved. There were probably corner-towers at both the south angles, and possibly platforms for *ballistae*—engines of war—at the north angles.

The foundations, and parts of the walling, of the central block of stone buildings were also well-preserved. They included the Headquarters Building, Officers' Quarters, two granaries and two other long buildings which may have been workshops or stores. Barracks of wood had stood in front and behind. There was one bath-house inside the north-east corner of the fort, and another outside the fort, in an annexe to east which was delimited by a ditch. The annexe bath-house had not been part of the original plan as it had been built over the fort's east ditches, and it may not have remained in use until the end of the Antonine occupation, since its walls had been levelled and covered with a spread of clay. From this and other stone buildings at Balmuildy Mr. Miller recovered evidence suggesting that there had been at least one destruction and one reoccupation of the fort.

From the ruins of the north gate there came fragments of another inscribed slab recording building work by the Second Legion in the governorship of Lollius Urbicus. No auxiliary cohort has so far been associated with Balmuildy.

Almost all the finds from the excavations could be assigned to the Antonine period. However, short-lived bronze coins of the late first century A.D. suggest a possible use of the site in the Agricolan period.

From the north gate of the fort a road ran north to the bank of the Kelvin, over 80 yards (72 m.) away, and the Military Way, after passing through the fort, turned north-west towards the river. Great Roman stone blocks from the abutments and piers of a bridge, and some wooden beams, possibly from its superstructure, were dredged up during the 1939-45 War from the bed of the river roughly on the line of the Military Way. Apparently Wall and Ditch stopped short on either bank of the river, leaving the bridge connecting the ends of the Military Way to close the gap in the frontier. In 1971 and 1974 the line of Wall and Ditch was determined outside the NW corner of the fort.

It has been suggested that Balmuildy, one of the only two stone-walled forts on the Antonine frontier, was one of the terminals of the Clyde valley road. Indeed, native traffic may have been permitted to cross the frontier at this point, under very strict control of course, and in that case a break in the Antonine Wall would be expected somewhere on the north bank of the Kelvin.

No sign of a break appears on the ground as the Wall and Ditch climb gently northwards from the valley of the Kelvin to Summerston Farm, making one sharp turn just north of the river and another north of the farm, close upon half a mile (·8 km.) from the river. The line is then crossed by the Glasgow-Balmore road. As it makes for the striking eminence of Crow Hill to the north-west, the hollow of the Ditch may be seen from the road running close to field boundaries. On Crow Hill, 200 feet (60 m.) above sea-level, the Roman line swings away very sharply south-westwards, and here, at the angle, a fortlet would be expected. Trenching in 1961 revealed the stone base of the Wall but did not discover a fortlet.

The Roman frontier may be re-joined by following the Balmore road north from Summerston, until a minor road branches off westwards, passing to the north of Crow Hill. As the Antonine Wall and Ditch are crossed by this minor road, Boclair Road (B8049), the hollow of the Ditch may be seen clearly on Douglas Park Golf Course. In 1976 the Wall base was located here.

A little farther westwards, in New Kilpatrick cemetery on the north side of Boclair Road, two well-preserved stretches of the stone base of the Wall are exposed to view. The base is here 14-15 feet (4·3-4·5 m.) wide. Each stretch has a gutter incorporated in it, and one stretch has a " step " in it to increase the stability of the turf superstructure.

NEW KILPATRICK OR BEARSDEN TO CASTLEHILL (Fig. 20)

From New Kilpatrick cemetery westwards to Bearsden, there are no remains to be seen of the Antonine frontier, although a modern road—Roman Road—almost certainly runs above the Military Way, at least for part of its length. The early antiquaries referred to the remains of a fort here, on the west side of the Allander Burn, on ground sloping north to the Manse Burn.

Excavations carried out from 1973-1978 by Dr. D. J. Breeze proved that the fort had an internal area of 2·3 acres (0·9 h.), and was defended by a turf rampart on a stone base c. 14 feet (4·3 m.) wide, by three ditches on the west side, and by one (uninterrupted) on the south side. The south ditch ran on eastwards to form the south ditch of an annexe attached to the fort on its east side and of about half its internal area. The annexe was defended by a turf rampart on a stone base, and had two east ditches (Fig. 20).

The Antonine Wall and Ditch formed the northern defences of the fort and annexe, averaging 14 feet (4·3 m.), and 20 feet (6 m.) wide respectively. There was no break in the Ditch opposite the north gate of the fort or annexe.

Buildings found within the fort, on the north and south sides of Roman Road, included two stone granaries, and, in timber, two or three barrack blocks, five or six long narrow buildings (possibly stables or store-houses), a workshop and other indeterminate buildings. There was apparently no headquarters building.

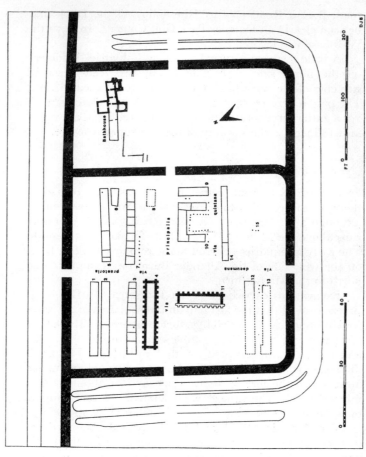

Key to the numbers:

1, 2, 5, 6 and ?12   stables or storehouses
3, 7 and ?13   barrack-blocks
4 and 11   granaries
9   storehouse
10   workshop
15   open space—works area?
8 and 14   unknown

In the annexe, there was a timber building just outside the east gate of the fort. Farther east, in the annexe, Dr. Breeze discovered a bath-house in exceptionally fine preservation. This has been consolidated for display as a permanent feature.

Finds from the excavations included a building inscription of the Twentieth Legion, the head of a goddess, possibly Fortuna, and many other artefacts. The pottery was all of Antonine date, with the exception of a few survivals. The Antonine fort at Bearsden had apparently only one period of occupation.

West of Roman Road, and its westward continuation Thorn Road, the Roman line turned north-west to make for high ground on the west side of Bearsden. Here in " Roman Park ", reached from a footpath connecting Milverton Avenue and Westbourne Crescent, there is a fairly well-preserved though tree-grown stretch of the Ditch. In 1963 excavation determined the exact line of Wall and Ditch between Bearsden and Castlehill. At Bearsden the Military Way seems to have sent off a by-pass whose line is now roughly continued by Upper Thorn Road and by a path across Bearsden Golf Course.

CASTLEHILL TO DUNTOCHER

Castlehill lies almost 400 feet (120 m.) above sea-level. It has one of the finest prospects of any fort-site on the Wall. Besides the view north to the hills and eastwards along the line, there was a wide outlook westwards and south-westwards over the estuary of the Clyde to the Renfrewshire coast.

The existence of a fort on Castlehill was indicated by the discovery of a column-capital in 1847 and of an altar, found in 1826, dedicated to the Spirits of the Campus and to Britannia by the commander of the Fourth Cohort of Gauls, 500 strong. More recently, Professor St. Joseph has observed from the air the south ditches and south-east angle of the fort. In 1970-4, Antonine pottery was found in the roots of fallen trees on the summit.

From Castlehill the Antonine Wall and Ditch swing south-west. The Ditch is in fairly good preservation, and serves as a field boundary, with a hedge planted in it, for part of the way between Castlehill and Hutcheson Hill. Just west of Castlehill the line is crossed by a modern road, the Peel Glen Road, and then crosses the Peel Burn, where the eighteenth-century antiquaries believed there had been a fortlet.

From Hutcheson Hill to the eastern slope of Golden Hill, Duntocher, the line of Wall and Ditch is closely accompanied by a modern road leading from Cleddans Farm to the Hardgate-Clydebank road (Cleddans Road). On the western slope of Hutcheson Hill, a fine distance slab of the Twentieth Legion was found in 1969 (Fig. 6.)

On the eastern slope of Golden Hill, the course of both Wall and Ditch was established in 1947 through excavation, before a housing scheme obliterated them. The Wall base was 16 feet (4·8 m.) wide, and the Ditch 20 feet (6 m.) wide.

GOLDEN HILL, DUNTOCHER TO OLD KILPATRICK (Fig. 21)

A Roman bath-house was discovered on the western slope of Golden Hill in the late eighteenth century, and a statuette of a woman, querns, pottery and coins were also recorded from the site. The location of the bath-house, north of Duntocher Trinity Parish Church, was confirmed in 1978. Excavations in what is now Golden Hill Park, between 1948 and 1951, showed that, before the Antonine Wall arrived, there had been an Antonine fortlet and a Antonine fort on the site. The fortlet, about 60 feet (18 m.) square, occupied the most commanding position on the Hill, which is about 200 feet (60 m.) above sea-level, and it was defended by a rampart 12 feet (3·6 m.) wide at the base, and by one ditch.

To this fortlet, on its east side, was later added a fort, with an internal area of ·5 acre (·2 h.), the smallest known fort on the Antonine Wall. It was defended by a rampart

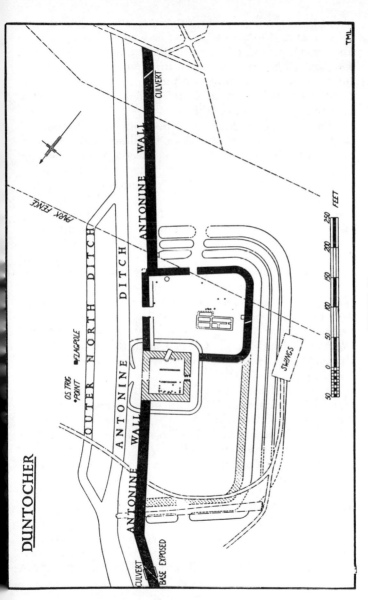

DUNTOCHER

FIGURE 21

about 13 feet (3·9 m.) wide at the base, and by three ditches on its east and south sides. On its west side there was an annexe, almost twice as large as the fort itself, enclosed by a rampart, with three ditches on the south side, and one on the west side. The tiny fort had no south gate, and the Military Way skirted the south defences, sending off a branch to the east gate of the fort.

The internal buildings had been much damaged, but there had been at least one stone building (perhaps a unit office) near the centre. Barracks of wood stood within the fortlet, later retained in use as a military enclosure attached to the fort, and in part at least of the interior of the fort.

When the Antonine Wall, 16 feet (4·8 m.) wide, was brought up to the east rampart of the fort, it made a very awkward junction with it about 10 feet (3 m.) south of the corner. The Antonine Ditch, 20 feet (6 m.) wide, was accompanied along the whole north front of both fort and annexe by an outer north ditch about 14 feet (4·3 m.) wide.

The excavations revealed evidence for alterations in plan at least once during the Antonine period. All the finds were of Antonine date. In 1977-8 the stone base of Duntocher fortlet was exposed to view by Clydebank District Council, and in 1979 the Council, with the co-operation of Dr. A. A. R. Henderson, created a " Roman Garden " north-west of the fort.

Just west of the fort on Golden Hill, the Antonine Wall and Ditch inclined slightly south to run down the hill to the Duntocher Burn, which was reached close to the modern bridge. (The inscribed slab set in the bridge, although in Latin, is of a recent date.)

On crossing the Duntocher Burn, the Antonine Wall made for the foothills of the Kilpatrick range, and clung precariously to them for well over a mile (1·6 km.) before swinging south to the Clyde. The Roman line on the western border of Duntocher is best approached by turning up a side road—Morrison Street—running northwards via Auchentoshan Avenue to Beeches Road. Between Duntocher Burn and Beeches Road, the line has not been precisely determined. In 1957, however, excavation in ground north of Beeches Road, before housing development took place, determined the line of the Ditch.

The course of Wall and Ditch is closely followed by the continuation westwards of Beeches Road and by a track running west from it past Carleith Farm. Just north of the track, in 1969 and 1971, the line of the Wall and Ditch was established by trenching.

Less than a mile (1·6 km.) to the west, at Mt. Pleasant Farm, the Wall and Ditch turned sharply south, to be ruthlessly cut across by the Glasgow-Dumbarton highway (A82), the road through Old Kilpatrick (A814) and a railway line.

OLD KILPATRICK (Fig. 22)

At the west end of Old Kilpatrick, partly under the houses of Gavinburn Gardens, is the site of the terminal fort at the west end of the Antonine Wall. Excavations carried out there by Mr. S. N. Miller in 1923-24, supplemented by trenching by Sir George Macdonald in 1931, have proved that before the Wall was built an Antonine fort had been established at Old Kilpatrick, doubtless to command the waterway of the Clyde. It had rounded corners on all four sides, and faced north-west.

This fort had an internal area of 4·2 acres (1·7 h.), and was at first defended by a rampart 14·5 feet (4·4 m.) wide at the base, by three ditches on its north and east sides, two on its south side and one on its west side. Later, the Antonine Wall was brought up to its north-west corner, and either then or subsequently, the number of ditches on north and east sides was increased to four, and on the west side to three (the Antonine Ditch here branching into three ditches). From the south-west corner of the fort, the Antonine Wall, accompanied by three ditches, continued south to the Clyde, about 150 yards (140 m.) away, cutting across as they did so the Military Way, which had earlier

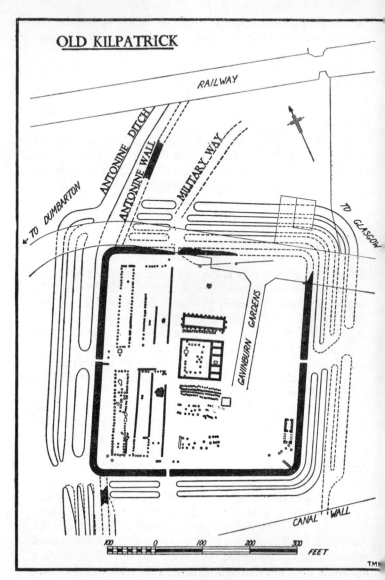

OLD KILPATRICK

RAILWAY

TO DUMBARTON

ANTONINE DITCH

ANTONINE WALL

MILITARY WAY

TO GLASGOW

GAVINBURN GARDENS

CANAL WALL

100 0 100 200 300 FEET

T.M.

FIGURE 22

continued westwards beyond the Roman frontier, probably to a supply base at or below Dumbarton.

Excavation in the interior of the fort revealed, in the centre, remains of the Headquarters Building, and a granary, both of stone, and three wooden buildings, perhaps a barn, workshops or stores. The post-holes or sleeper trenches of wooden barrack blocks were traced in front of the central block. To the south of the fort, between it and the river, there had been an annexe. Here, in the late eighteenth century, remains of a bath-house were found.

Mr. Miller recovered evidence suggesting that the Antonine fort had been destroyed and reoccupied at least once, and he also discovered slight structural remains which seemed possibly to have been earlier than the Antonine fort. A little pottery of late first-century date suggested, in any case, that Agricola had used this important site on the Clyde before it was called on to play a major role in the Antonine frontier system.

At the end of 1969, an altar to Jupiter Best and Greatest was found at Old Kilpatrick. It had been dedicated by the First Cohort of Baetasii, known to have been stationed for a time at Bar Hill.

A visitor to the Antonine Wall who walks south down Gavinburn Place to the Canal, and turns right, will enjoy a magnificent view down the Firth of Clyde. He will also be standing at the most north-westerly corner of the Roman Empire.

BIBLIOGRAPHY

Abbreviations in use are: *DES*, Discovery and Excavation, Scotland; *GAJ*, Glasgow Archaeological Journal; *JRS*, Journal of Roman Studies; *PSAS*, Proceedings of the Society of Antiquaries of Scotland; *SAF*, Scottish Archaeological Forum.

General

The most comprehensive publication on the Antonine Wall, is Sir George Macdonald's *Roman Wall in Scotland* (2nd ed. 1934). See also the O.S. $2\frac{1}{2}$ in. map of the Antonine Wall, 1969.

GLASGOW ARCHAEOLOGICAL SOCIETY. *The Antonine Wall Report*, 1899.

BIRLEY, A. R.   Roman Frontiers and Roman Frontier Policy, *Trans. Archit. and Archaeol. Soc. of Durham and Northumberland*, 3 (1974), 13 ff.

BIRLEY, E.   *Roman Britain and the Roman Army*, 1953.

BREEZE, D. J.   The Abandonment of the Antonine Wall: its Date and Implications, *SAF* 7 (1975), 67 ff.
The Line of the Antonine Wall at Falkirk, *PSAS* 106 (1975), 200 ff.

BREEZE, D. J. and DOBSON, B.   The Development of the Mural Frontier in Britain from Hadrian to Caracalla, *PSAS* 102 (1970), 109 ff.
A View of Roman Scotland in 1975, *GAJ* 4 (1976), 124 ff.

CURLE, J.   An Inventory of Objects of Roman and Provincial Roman Origin found on Sites in Scotland not definitely associated with Roman Constructions, *PSAS* 66 (1932), 277 ff.

DAVIES, R. W.   A Lost Inscription from Auchendavy, *GAJ* 4 (1976), 103 ff.

DISCOVERY AND EXCAVATION, SCOTLAND (*DES*), 1955-1978, continuing.   (For discoveries and excavations on the line of the Antonine Wall.)

GILLAM, J. P.   Sources of Pottery found on Northern Military Sites, in Detsicas, A. (ed.), *Current Research in Romano-British Coarse Pottery*, 1963, 53 ff.
Possible Changes in Plan in the Course of the Construction of the Antonine Wall, *SAF* 7 (1975), 51 ff.
Coarse Fumed Ware in North Britain and Beyond, *GAJ* 4 (1976), 57 ff.

GILLAM, J. P. and MANN, J. C.   The Northern British Frontier from Antoninus Pius to Caracalla, *Arch. Ael.* (4), 48 (1970), 1 ff.

HARTLEY, B.   The Roman Occupations of Scotland: the Evidence of Samian Ware, *Britannia* 3 (1972), 1 ff.

HARTLEY, KATHARINE. Were Mortaria made in Roman
   Scotland?, *GAJ* 4 (1976), 81 ff.
HENDRY, T. A. Antonine Wall Excavations: Kinneil
   Sector, *GAJ* 2 (1971), 107 ff.
KEPPIE, L. J. F. The Building of the Antonine Wall:
   Archaeological and Epigraphic Evidence, *PSAS*
   105 (1974), 151 ff.
   The Distance Slabs from the Antonine Wall:
   Some Problems, *SAF* 7 (1975), 57 ff.
   Legio II Augusta and the North Gate at Bal-
   muildy, *GAJ* 4 (1976), 99 ff.
   Some Rescue Excavations on the Line of the
   Antonine Wall, 1973-6, *PSAS* 107 (1976), 61 ff.
   Roman Distance Slabs from the Antonine Wall, 1979.
MACDONALD, G. Discoveries on the Line of the Antonine
   Wall, *PSAS* 49 (1915), 93 ff.; 59 (1925), 270 ff.
   The Building of the Antonine Wall, *JRS* 11 (1921),
   1 ff. Roman Coins Found in Scotland, *PSAS* 52
   (1918), 203 ff.; 58 (1924), 325 ff.; 68 (1934),
   27 ff.; 73 (1939), 241 ff.
MACDONALD, J. *Tituli Hunteriani:* An Account of the
   Roman Stones in the Hunterian Museum, Univer-
   sity of Glasgow, 1897.
MAIN, LORNA. Inveravon Farm, *PSAS* 107 (1976), 61 f.
MANN, J. C. The Raising of New Legions during the
   Principate, *Hermes* 91 (1963), 483 ff.
MAXWELL, G. S. The Building of the Antonine Wall,
   *Actes du IXe Congrès International sur les Frontières
   Romaines*, 1974, 327 ff; and in *RCAHM, Lanarkshire*.
RICHMOND, I. A. ed. *Roman and Native in North Britain*, 1958.
ROBERTSON, ANNE S. Roman Coins found in Scotland,
   PSAS 84 (1950), 137 ff.; 94 (1961), 133 ff.; 103
   (1971), 113 ff.
   A Hoard of Roman Silver Coins from Briglands,
   Rumbling Bridge, Kinross-shire, *PSAS* 90 (1957),
   241 ff.
   Miscellanea Romano-Caledonica, *PSAS* 97 (1964),
   180 ff.

Recent Work on the Antonine Wall, *GAJ* 1 (1969), 37 ff.

Roman Finds from Non-Roman Sites in Scotland, *Britannia* 1 (1970), 198 ff.

River Crossings on the Antonine Wall, in *Roman Frontier Studies* 1969 (1974), 94 ff.

The Romans in North Britain: The Coin Evidence, in Temporini, H. (ed.) *Aufstieg und Niedergang der römischen Welt*, 11, iii (1975), 364 ff.

Agricola's Campaigns in Scotland and their Aftermath, *SAF* 7 (1975), 1 ff.

The Circulation of Coins in North Britain: the Evidence of Hoards and Site Finds from Scotland, in Carson, R. A. G. and Kraay, C. M. (ed.), *Essays Presented to Humphrey Sutherland*, 1978, 186 ff.

SKINNER, D. *The Countryside of the Antonine Wall* (Countryside Commission for Scotland), 1973.

SMITH, S. Notes on an Artificial Mound at Bonnybridge, *PSAS* 68 (1934), 59 ff.

The Antonine Wall and Ditch near Bonnybridge, *PSAS* 70 (1936), 146 f.

STEER, K. A. The Antonine Wall, 1934-1959, *JRS* 50 (1960), 84 ff.

Excavations on the Antonine Wall in Polmont Park, and at Dean House, in 1960, *PSAS* 94 (1961), 322 ff.

Roman Monuments, *RCAHM, Stirlingshire*, 1963, 1, 93 ff.

John Horsley and the Antonine Wall, *Arch. Ael.* (4) 42 (1964), 1 ff.

Roman Monuments, *RCAHM, Lanarkshire*, 1978, 30 ff., 111 ff. (ed.)

STEER, K. A. and CORMACK, E. A. A New Roman Distance Slab from the Antonine Wall, *PSAS* 101 (1969), 122 ff.

WILSON, D. R. *Roman Frontiers of Britain*, 1967.

Air Reconnaissance and Roman Military Antiquities in Britain, *SAF* 7 (1975), 13 ff.

FORTS

Balmuildy

MILLER, S. N. *The Roman Fort at Balmuildy*, 1922.
STEER, K. A. (ed.), in *RCAHM, Lanarkshire*, 1978, 114 ff.

Bar Hill

MACDONALD, G. and PARK A. *The Roman Forts on the Bar Hill*, 1906.
ROBERTSON, ANNE S., SCOTT, MARGARET and KEPPIE, L. J. F. *Bar Hill: A Roman Fort and its Finds* (British Archaeological Report 16), 1975.

Bearsden

BREEZE, D. J. *The Roman Fort at Bearsden: 1973 Excavations, an interim report*, 1974; also in *DES* 1973, 63; 1974, 80; 1975, 20; 1976, 29; 1977, 12; 1978, 25 f.

Bridgeness and Carriden

MACDONALD, G. Bridgeness, *PSAS* 71 (1937), 383 ff.
ST. JOSEPH, J. K. S. Carriden, *PSAS*, 83 (1949), 167 ff.
RICHMOND, I. A. and STEER, K. A. *Castellum Veluniate* and Civilians on a Roman Frontier, *PSAS* 90 (1957), 1 ff.

Cadder

CLARKE, J. *The Roman Fort at Cadder*, 1933.
STEER, K. A. (ed.), in *RCAHM, Lanarkshire*, 1978, 121 ff.

Castlecary

CHRISTISON, D. and BUCHANAN, M. Excavation of Castlecary Fort, *PSAS* 37 (1903), 271 f.
STEER, K. A., in *RCAHM, Stirlingshire*, 1963, 1, 103 ff.

Croy Hill

MACDONALD, G. Croy Hill, *PSAS* 59 (1925), 288 ff.; 66 (1932), 243 ff.; 71 (1937), 32 ff.
HANSON, W. S., in *DES* 1975, 21 f.; 1976, 28; 1977, 12; 1978, 27.

Duntocher

ROBER[_ _]N, ANNE S. *An Antonine Fort: Golden Hill,*
  L   tocher, 1957.

Inveravon

ROB[_]RTSON, ANNE S. A Small Fort at Inveravon, West
  Lothian, *GAJ* 1 (1969), 39 ff.

Kirkintilloch

M[_]CDONALD, G. Kirkintilloch Fort, *PSAS* 59 (1925), 290 ff.
R[_]BERTSON, ANNE S. The Antonine Wall and Fort at
  Kirkintilloch, 1952-1961, *PSAS* 97 (1964), 180 ff.

Mumrills

MACDONALD, G. The Roman Fort at Mumrills, *PSAS* 63
  (1929), 396 ff.
  A New Inscription at Mumrills, *PSAS* 73 (1939),
  245 f.
ROBERTSON, ANNE S. A Roman Oven at Mumrills,
  Falkirk, *PSAS* 76 (1942), 119 ff.
SMITH, S. An Indeterminate Structure and a Hearth found
  outside the Roman Fort at Mumrills, *PSAS* 73
  (1939), 319 ff.
STEER, K. A. Excavations at Mumrills Fort 1958-60, *PSAS*
  94 (1961), 86 ff.; and in *RCAHM, Stirlingshire,*
  1963, 1, 96 ff.

Old Kilpatrick

MILLER, S. N. *The Roman Fort at Old Kilpatrick*, 1928.
MACDONALD, G. Old Kilpatrick, *PSAS* 66 (1932), 220 ff.

Rough Castle

BUCHANAN, M. Excavation of Rough Castle, *PSAS* 39
  (1905), 442 ff.
MACDONALD, G. Rough Castle Fort, *PSAS* 59 (1925),
  285 ff.; 67 (1933), 244 ff.
MACIVOR, I., in *JRS*, 1959, 104; 1962, 163.
STEER, K. A., in *RCAHM, Stirlingshire*, 1963, 1, 100 ff.

KEPPIE, L. J. F.   Excavation of Roman Sites at
    Dullatur and Westerwood, *GAJ* 5 (1979), 9 ff.
MACDONALD, G.   Westerwood, *PSAS* 67 (1933), 277 ff.
    (See also *DES* 1963, 49 f.; *JRS* 1964, 178; *PSAS*
    100 (1968), 192 f.; *DES* 1974, 81; 1975, 21;
    1978, 27.)

FORT-ANNEXES

RICHMOND, I. A. and STEER, K. A.   *Castellum Veluniate*, and
    Civilians on a Roman Frontier, *PSAS* 90 (1957),
    1 ff.

FORTLETS

BREEZE, D. J.   Excavations at the Roman Fortlet on the
    Antonine Wall at Watling Lodge, 1972-1974,
    PSAS 105, 1974, 166 ff.
HANSON, W. S., in *DES* 1977, 12 f. (Croy Hill fortlet).
HANSON, W. S. and KEPPIE, L. J. F.   Seabegs Wood and
    Croy Hill, in *Current Archaeology*, 62 (June 1978),
    91 ff.
ROBERTSON, ANNE S.   *An Antonine Fort: Golden Hill*,
    Duntocher, 1957.
ST. JOSEPH, J. K. S., in *JRS* 1951, 61; 1955, 86 (Glasgow
    Bridge and Wilderness).
STEER, K. A. (ed.), in *RCAHM, Lanarkshire*, 1978, 134
    (Glasgow Bridge), 136 f. (Wilderness).
WILKES, J. J.   The Antonine Fortlet at Wilderness Planta-
    tion, Lanarkshire, *GAJ* 3 (1974), 51 ff.

SIGNALLING PLATFORMS

STEER, K. A.   The Nature and Purpose of the Expansions
    on the Antonine Wall, *PSAS* 90 (1957), 161 ff.;
    also in *RCAHM, Stirlingshire*, 1963, 1, 95 f., and (ed.)
    in *RCAHM, Lanarkshire*, 1978, 38, 112 f.

Temporary Camps

Feachem, R. W.   Six Roman Camps near the Antonine Wall, *PSAS* 89 (1956), 329 ff.   (See also under *Aerial Discoveries*.)

Keppie, L. J. F.   Evcavation of Roman Sites at Dullatur and Westerwood, *GAJ* 5 (1979) 9 ff.

The Western Flank

Feachem, R. W., in *JRS*, 43 (1953), 105, 107, figs. 24, 25 (Lurg Moor).

Newall, F.   The Roman Signal Fortlet at Outerwards, Ayrshire, *GAJ* 4 (1976), 111 ff.

Steer, K. A.   The Roman Fort at Whitemoss, Renfrewshire (Bishopton), *PSAS* 83 (1949), 28 ff.

Aerial Discoveries

St. Joseph, J. K. S., in *JRS* 41 (1951), 61 f.; 45 (1955), 86 f.; 48 (1958), 89 f.; 51 (1961), 122 f.; 55 (1965), 80; 59 (1969), 104 ff.; 67 (1977), 134 f. Air Reconnaissance of Roman Scotland, 1939-75, *GAJ* 4 (1976), 1 ff.

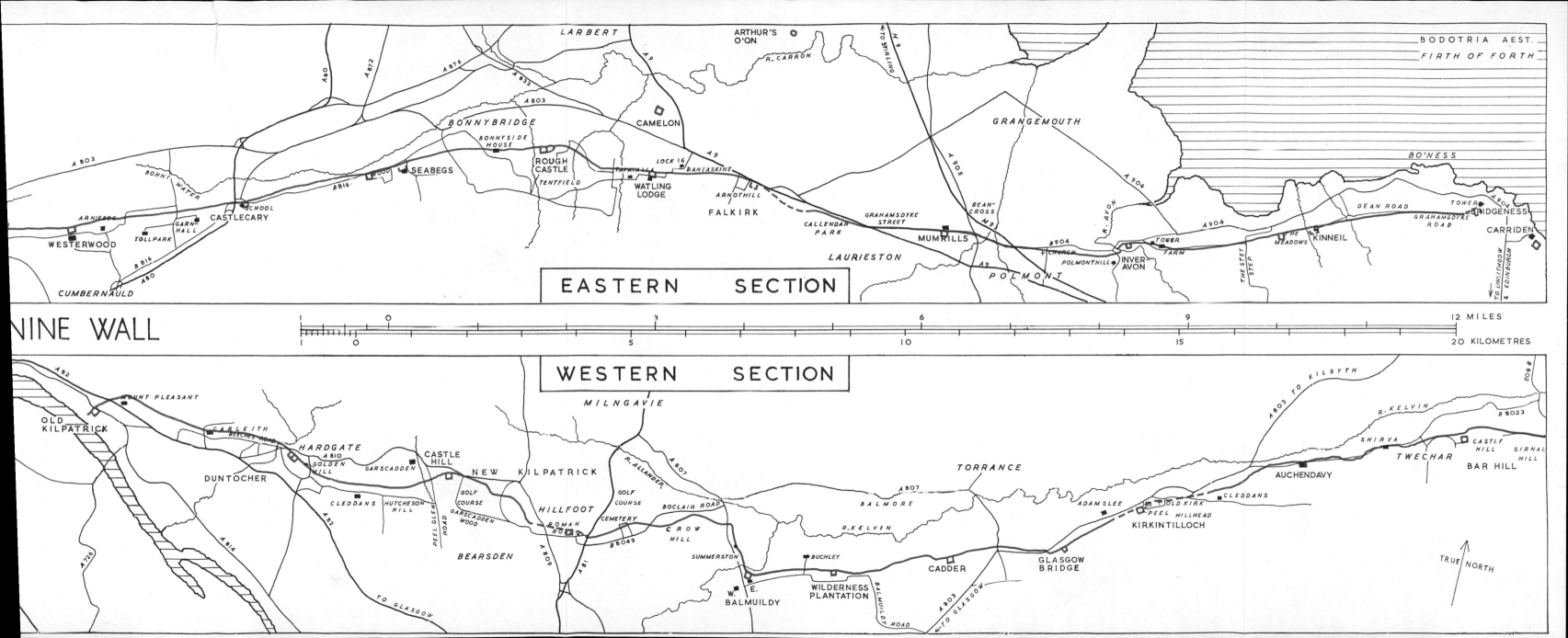

ARTHUR'S O'ON

LARBERT

BODOTRIA AEST.
FIRTH OF FORTH

R. CARRON

TO STIRLING

M 9

GRANGEMOUTH

BO'NESS

A 80
A 872
A 876
A 833

A 803

BONNYBRIDGE

BONNYSIDE HOUSE

CAMELON

A 803

A 9

A 9

A 905

A 904

DEAN ROAD

A 904

TOWER

A 803

BONNI WATER

WOOD

B 816

SEABEGS

ROUGH CASTLE

TATAVALLA

LOCK 16

BANTASKINE

BEAN-CROSS

M 9

BRIDGENESS

TENTFIELD

WATLING LODGE

ARNOTHILL

A 904

GRAHAMSDYKE ROAD

ARNIEBOG

SCHOOL

CASTLECARY

FALKIRK

GRAHAMSDYKE STREET

R. AVON

TOWER FARM

THE MEADOWS

KINNEIL

GRAHAMSDYKE ROAD

CARRIDEN

GARN-HALL

CALLENDAR PARK

MUMRILLS

A 904

CHURCH

A 904

WESTERWOOD

TOLLPARK

B 816

LAURIESTON

POLMONTHILL

INVER-AVON

THE STEY STEP

TO LINLITHGOW & EDINBURGH

A 80

A 9

POLMONT

CUMBERNAULD

EASTERN SECTION

ANTONINE WALL

| 1 | | | 0 | | | 3 | | | 6 | | | 9 | | | 12 MILES |

| 1 | | 0 | | 5 | | | 10 | | | 15 | | | 20 KILOMETRES |

WESTERN SECTION

A 82

MOUNT PLEASANT

MILNGAVIE

A 803 TO KILSYTH

B 8023

R. KELVIN

OLD KILPATRICK

CARLEITH

BEECHES ROAD

HARDGATE

A 810

GOLDEN HILL

CASTLE HILL

GARSCADDEN

NEW KILPATRICK

R. ALLANDER

A 807

TORRANCE

SHIRVA

CASTLE HILL

GIRNAL HILL

DUNTOCHER

CLEDDANS

HUTCHESON HILL

GOLF COURSE

HILLFOOT

GOLF COURSE

BOCLAIR ROAD

A 807

BALMORE

TWECHAR

BAR HILL

AUCHENDAVY

PEEL GLEN ROAD

GARSCADDEN WOOD

ROMAN ROAD

CEMETERY

B 8049

CROW HILL

R. KELVIN

ADAMSLEE

OLD KIRK

CLEDDANS

BEARSDEN

A 809

A 81

SUMMERSTON

BUCHLEY

CADDER

PEEL HILLHEAD

KIRKINTILLOCH

A 726

A 814

TO GLASGOW

W. E. BALMUILDY

WILDERNESS PLANTATION

BALMUILDY ROAD

A 803 TO GLASGOW

GLASGOW BRIDGE

TRUE NORTH

MUSEUMS OPEN TO THE PUBLIC IN WHICH MATERIAL FROM THE ANTONINE WALL IS PRESERVED

NATIONAL MUSEUM OF ANTIQUITIES,
QUEEN STREET, EDINBURGH.

Weekdays 10 *to* 5, *Sunday* 2 *to* 5. *Free.*

Distance slab from Bridgeness; other building stones, altars and tombstones from the Antonine Wall; finds from the excavation of the forts at Mumrills, Rough Castle, and Castlecary, and a few finds from Croy Hill and Cadder.

HUNTERIAN MUSEUM,
UNIVERSITY OF GLASGOW.

Monday to Friday 9 *to* 5, *Saturday* 9 *to* 12 *noon. Free.*

All but two of the surviving distance slabs; other building stones, altars and tombstones from the Antonine Wall; finds from the excavation of the forts at Castlecary, Croy Hill, Bar Hill, Kirkintilloch, Cadder, Balmuildy, Bearsden, Duntocher and Old Kilpatrick; from Inveravon, Seabegs and Wilderness; models of the Antonine Wall, and Balmuildy fort, etc.

MUSEUM AND ART GALLERY,
KELVINGROVE, GLASGOW.

Weekdays 10 *to* 5, *Sunday* 2 *to* 5. *Free.*

Distance slab from East Millichen; models of forts on the Antonine Wall.

FALKIRK MUSEUM

Weekdays 10 *to* 12.30, 1.30 *to* 5. *Free.*

Altar from Westerwood; finds from Mumrills, Rough Castle, Castlecary.

THE AULD KIRK MUSEUM, KIRKINTILLOCH.

Tuesdays, Thursdays, Saturdays, 1.30 to 4.45 p.m., and by arrangement. Free.

Finds from Bar Hill and Kirkintilloch.

THE MOST IMPRESSIVE FEATURES ON THE LINE OF THE ANTONINE WALL

THE STONE BASE OF THE WALL	Preserved in New Kilpatrick Cemetery, (p. 83).
THE TURF SUPERSTRUCTURE	West of Rough Castle, (p. 56).
THE DITCH	Callendar Park, (p. 50). Bantaskine, (p. 51). Watling Lodge, (p. 52). Tentfield Plantation, (p. 53). Rough Castle, (pp. 53 ff.). Seabegs Wood, (p. 57 f). Garnhall, (p. 61). Westerwood, (p. 62). Dullatur, (p. 54). Croy Hill, (pp. 65 ff.). Bar Hill, (p. 69).
THE FORT AT ROUGH CASTLE	pp. 53 ff.
THE FORT AT BAR HILL	pp. 69 ff.
THE BATHHOUSE AT BEARSDEN	p. 85.

ANTONINE WALL

(Stretches in Public Ownership)

In Care of Secretary of State for Scotland

Watling Lodge NS 866798-863798
Rough Castle NS 845800-835798
Seabegs Wood NS 815794-811792
Castlecary NS 791784-778781
Garnhall NS 784781-778779
Tollpark NS 778779-769777
Dullatur NS 756773-751772
Croy Hill NS 738769-725762
Bar Hill NS 713762-706759

Owned by Local Authorities

Kinneil (Falkirk) NS 987806-976804
Polmonthill (Falkirk) NS 950795-944792
Callendar Park (Falkirk) NS 901795-892796
Tollpark-Arniebog (Cumbernauld and Kilsyth)
    NS 778779-764774
Kirkintilloch Fort (Strathkelvin) NS 651740
New Kilpatrick Cemetery (Bearsden and Milngavie)
    NS 757723 and 756723
Thorn Road, Bearsden (Bearsden and Milngavie)
    NS 535724-532724
Hutcheson Hill (Glasgow) NS 517724-514723
Duntocher Fort (Clydebank) NS 495726

FOOTNOTE

Grateful acknowledgement is made of the assistance given in the proof-reading by Mr. L. J. F. Keppie, and Miss Isobel J. Robertson.

INDEX

PRINTED IN GREAT BRITAIN BY T. AND A. CONSTABLE LTD., EDINBURGH